GHOST INVESTIGATOR

Volume 11

Written by
Linda Zimmermann

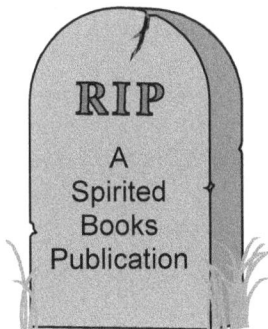

RIP

A
Spirited
Books
Publication

Linda Zimmermann's Facebook Fan Page

http://www.facebook.com/pages/Linda-Zimmermann/116636310250

The author is always looking for new ghost stories. If you would like to share a haunting experience or find out more about her work, go to:

www.ghostinvestigator.com

Or write to:

Linda Zimmermann
P.O. Box 192
Blooming Grove, NY 10914

Or send email to:

lindazim@optonline.net

What else is Linda Zimmermann writing? Go to: **www.gotozim.com**

Ghost Investigator: Volume 11

ISBN: 978-1-937174-00-2

CONTENTS

Author's Note

It's been another fascinating year of discovery and adventure.

At the end of February, I went to the International UFO Congress in Arizona to debut my book about UFOs in the Hudson Valley, *In the Night Sky*. Big Guy Media made a documentary about my research, and director Felix Olivieri was there at the film festival—and the film won the People's Choice Award by a landslide! It was like winning an Alien Oscar. My research into UFOs continues, and a new book will be coming out soon.

Also this year, research on another book project has begun. My ghost hunting partner, Michael Worden, and I are tracking down, and trekking to, *Mysterious Stone Sites of the Hudson Valley* (see the Facebook page of this name for more info and photos). There are countless standing stones, cairns, walls, chambers, perched boulders, and calendar stone sites throughout the area, and far too many have been bulldozed or dismissed as the work of colonial farmers. We hope to identify many of these sites, and raise awareness of them so that they might be preserved and studied. (And we also just love to run around the woods uncovering new mysteries!)

Of course, the one constant that has been part of my life for over a decade and a half, is my ghost investigations. There's still nothing like that adrenaline rush of arriving at a haunted site, and wondering what awaits us in the darkness and stillness of the night. I was fortunate to get into some amazing historic sites, houses, and even a haunted library this year.

In *Ghost Investigator Volume 11*, I have also included something new—well, really very old—a chapter on ghost stories that appeared in newspapers from the 19th and early 20th centuries. A friend had given me a couple of old newspaper clippings, which sparked a deep interest, so I spent a lot of time combing through archives to find these stories, and I think it was worth the time. If skeptics claim that ghostly encounters are an invention of modern media, they had better think again, as I was able to find articles dating back to the 1870s.

And rest assured I am already working on new cases for Volume 12. As long as the dead aren't resting, I won't, either!

Linda Zimmermann
September 2013

Emma Martin House
Bloomingburg, NY

Jane Connor owns a lovely white house in Bloomingburg, NY; a house that has been in her family since 1920. Of course, appearances can be deceiving, as there are mysteries here which have left a palpable pall across the property. What happened on this ground before the house was built? What secrets did the original owner keep hidden from the world? How have Jane's own family members added to the many layers of unusual activity that takes place within these walls?

What Jane knows for sure about the history of the house is that it was built in the Folk Victorian style between 1900-1902 by the widow of a Civil War veteran—Emma L. Littell Martin. Emma was born in 1847, and her husband, Francis Martin (1841-1897), was a Scottish immigrant who met Emma in Brooklyn. They bought a farm in the town of Wallkill, and lived there with their son, George, and a farmhand, Alexander Johnson, who was most likely born into slavery in Virginia in 1855. When Francis passed away, George took over the farm, and Emma bought the piece of property on which her house was built.

Emma lived in the house with Alexander until her death in 1913. Many years ago, a neighbor (Ethel Goudy, who was the postmistress of Bloomingburg) told Jane's father that she was six when she watched the house being built, and recalled Emma standing on the property watching every board being put in place—and if there was a knot or imperfection in the wood she insisted on another piece. Ethel also remembers Emma being rather closemouthed and private.

Jane believes that Emma was very close with Alexander, which has left her wondering just what kind of the relationship they shared—but more on that bit of paranormal gossip later.

When Emma passed away, her son took over ownership of the house, and he sold it to a couple named Easeman, but they only kept the house for a couple of years. They sold the property to Jane's grandmother, Mary Albright Post. Mary came from a wealthy family in Philadelphia, but married William H. Post, who managed to spend all of her money. They had three children, one of whom was Jane's father, Townsend.

Unfortunately, Mary's brother was a soldier in WWI who contracted tuberculosis in the army. When he came home, Mary became infected and died a slow and painful death. She was apparently gasping for her final breaths as she was taken away to a hospital, but it was too late. Her husband, William, would also later pass away of a respiratory illness; pneumonia in 1963. Perhaps not surprisingly, one of the inexplicable sounds in the house is of someone wheezing.

(In an interesting bit of trivia, Jane has photos of her grandmother when she was at the Trudeau Sanatorium in Saranac Lake, NY, and Dr. Trudeau's descendant is Garry Trudeau, the famous *Doonesbury* cartoonist.)

I asked who had experienced the earliest unusual activity in the house, and the first incident Jane is aware of is something her mother encountered in the 1970s. While standing in the kitchen, she saw a face glaring at her through a small window. It was a man's face and the skin was very tan. He had green eyes, an earring, and gave the overall appearance of being a sailor. The face seemed to just float there, and then vanished.

Jane's mother also saw soldiers with weapons in the backyard that were "coming up over the hill," but she couldn't identify the uniforms.

Jane's brother was an amateur photographer and was taking photos of flowers and trees in the backyard in the 1980s. When he developed the film, he was stunned to see that in one of the pictures there was a man in uniform standing in the yard. The photo greatly upset him, and he threw it in a box and put it in storage, and unfortunately it is now lost.

Had there been some sort of encampment or battle on this land? Jane sometimes asks questions out loud to see if there are any responses, and when she asked if there were soldiers on the property, there was a distinct knocking sound. When she asked if there were any bodies buried there, there was another knock. I asked if anyone had ever used a metal detector on the property, and she said no, so I made a mental note that someday I would like to return and do some real field work with my detector.

After Jane's mother passed away in 2000, her father—a complete skeptic—told her that he kept hearing the sounds of a woman crying and footsteps.

"Jane, this house is haunted," he declared one day, much to her surprise.

Her father continued to hear all kinds of strange sounds, most often footsteps, but sometimes they were so loud it was like the furniture was being moved. Although Jane wasn't hearing everything her father claimed to be experiencing, she and her son decided to put an audio recorder upstairs, and they found that they had captured what sounded like a woman walking in high-heeled shoes. And that was just the start of recording countless EVPs and odd noises that have continued for all these years.

When Jane's father passed away in the house in 2008, activity really picked up—or at least Jane now became the focal point for the activity. In addition to all the many sounds, she actually saw a white figure around five feet tall rush by the dining room doorway, saw another figure that was undulating "like steam rising," felt someone sit down on the bed, and has felt a "whoosh" of air on several occasion. She has also found pennies on the floor. Of course, people do drop change, but this was most unusual—there were five pennies lined up on the bathroom floor, and no one else was home.

Much of the activity takes place in the attic, where Jane heard her cat meowing—six months after it had died, and someone during another investigation was pushed. I asked why she thought the attic was such a paranormal hotspot, and Jane replied that she felt that Alexander had secretly lived up in the attic, and that he and Emma had been lovers! Of course it is all speculation, but wouldn't that scenario have provided all kinds of fodder for a haunting!

When the carpeting was being replaced in the house, the workmen told Jane that the house was haunted. Among the unnerving things they experienced, was the front door which would close and lock on its own whenever they would go out to their truck and then try to get back in the house.

In the fall of 2011, a woman from Florida was visiting friends across the street. The woman told her friends that she saw someone standing by a window in Jane's house at night, while Jane was at work. She described the woman as being thin, having dark hair styled up on her head, and looking to be in her thirties. She was able to see such detail as Jane keeps electric candles in the windows, and the figure was illuminated. An

5

interesting note: weight loss is common in those suffering from tuberculosis, and Jane's grandmother was in her thirties when she died of the disease.

Another sighting occurred in the same kitchen window in which Jane's mother saw the face of the tanned man. Only now it was Jane who saw a man looking in, and it was her father! Her father was also seen by another woman, and this time he was sitting on the front porch. A third sighting occurred when a friend was driving by the house. She saw a man standing on the lawn by the porch and realized it looked just like Jane's deceased father. The woman slammed on the brakes and then quickly backed up to get a closer look, but the figure had vanished.

Jane Connor

There were many other stories of people who have seen, heard and sensed things in this house. Many people have an inexplicable fear of the attic. Several have requested the "buddy system" when using the bathroom—making sure someone was outside the door at all times. So clearly this is not the type of activity that limits itself to a certain time or to certain people—it is an equal opportunity haunting!

After sitting at the dining room table listening to the stories and taking notes, it was time to do a walkthrough and familiarize myself with the place. Switching on my EMF meter, I stood up and hadn't gone more than two steps before I started getting some rather high readings. As I was near a modern radio (made to look like an antique), I assumed that was the source of the EMF. However, the readings persisted even after I unplugged the radio, so that couldn't have been what was generating the EMF.

Next stop was the living room and the spot where her father had died by the couch. I asked Jane if it was okay to take a picture and she said it was, but apparently it wasn't okay with everyone, as I depressed the button on my camera and it didn't do anything. I pushed the button again, and still nothing happened. Finally, the third time the camera slowly and reluctantly took a picture. (The battery was fully charged and I always test everything before an investigation, so I have no explanation for this.)

We then looked at the many family photos of her parents and grandparents, and I couldn't help thinking what psychic Barbara Bleitzhofer would be able to "see" in those photos. Then there was the portrait of her grandfather, who was a rare book dealer in Greenwich Village, and had quite an interesting collection of friends who were actors and from the arts world. While it's a nice portrait of a man with a pleasant demeanor, I didn't exactly get a warm and fuzzy feeling about the man, and I would later find my instincts were correct, but more on that to follow.

We headed upstairs to her mother's former bedroom.

"I won't sleep in here!" Jane exclaimed. "There's always knocking and banging sounds. I was touched several times. And one time someone whispered my name."

Jane's grandfather

One night her grandson was sleeping in the room, and he heard a voice saying, "Come downstairs with me." He looked all around, but no one was there.

That would be enough to keep me from sleeping in that room, too! I checked the room with the EMF meter, and there were some high readings over her mother's bed.

The bathroom didn't feel particularly creepy, although the lights on the EMF meter went up and down a couple of times without me moving, so something was moving back and forth.

Next stop was Jane's bedroom, where she described some very loud, threatening sounds, and an object falling off the wall and hitting her in the face while she was in bed. There was also a dark hand reaching for her face. This had been the same room where her father and other family members had slept, and I wondered out loud why former family members would be responsible for such violent behavior toward one of their descendants.

"I think there are family members here," Jane said, "but there's also something very angry."

Who that angry person was, was yet to be determined.

Jane also talked about times she would hear the sounds of a struggle, with objects crashing to the ground and glass breaking, but then wouldn't find anything out of place. We discussed the possibility of this being some sort of "tape loop" of some act of violence in the past that left a deep imprint on the house. At the very least, it was clear there are mysteries in the house.

In her grandmother's old room, some friends had heard the sounds of heavy, labored breathing. There have also been the sounds of knocking coming from the closet.

We went up to the attic where there were more high EMF readings. I made sure to check where the electrical service was coming in, but that didn't account for the readings in many different spots. Once again, it took three tries to get my camera to take a picture. (It was fine everywhere else in the house and yard.) Jane pointed out where there had been a fire in the early 1900s, and part of the roof had been replaced. I took notes on everything, as you never knew what might be important later on.

We came downstairs so I could "gear up" and get my coat on to go back up to the attic to spend some time. With my digital recorder going I attempted an EVP session, asking questions about who might be there and why. While listening to the recording later, I did hear a faint man's voice yelling when I asked if a crime had been committed here, but as there were some people across the street sledding and playing in the snow, I couldn't rule out that one of them had shouted loud enough for my recorder to pick up.

While nothing dramatic happened on this initial meeting and walkthrough, there were enough tantalizing sounds, EMF readings, and fleeting impressions that this place did indeed have some dark secrets—and there's nothing more compelling in ghost hunting than that!

When I got home, I sent Barb a photo of the house (without telling her anything about it, not even where it was) just to see what her initial impressions might be. The following is her response and Jane's reaction:

Barb's email:

Ok, Very nice looking home.
Feels like a lot of people come & go, almost feels like a "stop" place to
rest up & move on.
It's funny, cause I keep hearing "the looks of the house are so beautiful,
but don't let it fool you"
I smell coffee, tea, "Earl Gray"& cookies?
The older woman was a saint, she says, "it was him"
I also keep hearing a different voice, like a "Dutch" voice. When I say
German, I see wooden shoes.
A woman keeps saying, "the man, the man, it's him, not me"
You know, I keep wanting to turn this house around in the photo & look at
the back. It's the back area that had the wild times.
Linda, feels like a few stories in this house & the house knows it. It's like
the house makes you fall in love with it & sucks you in.
What's with the kitchen cabinets? Long hallway?
They need to watch the railing on the top. Loose?? "relatives, they stay
close"... " Can't wait"... this almost sounds like it's coming from a girl?
Oh boy, did someone hang themself in there or out back?
"Pretty on the outside, different on the inside" & then he laughs...this man
is not cool.
Wow, let me know, Would love to see more photos if you have them. Is it
near you?
Hope this helps.

Jane's response:

Yes--according to my dad there were parties here years ago--My
grandfather had a rare book store in Little Bohemia aka Greenwich
Village and invited people from there to house parties--the children had to
give up their beds to the adults--as my father would say. My grandmother
Mary would be the saint--my grandfather was described as a real bastard.
I have often felt that I needed to hang on to the railing in the attic because
I might be pushed--That did happen to my one guest as she ascended the
staircase and went around the end of the railing. I think I mentioned that

11

during the interview. Another friend of mine voiced the same fear of being shoved without anyone telling her what happened. Feel free to come whenever you want with Barbara --BTW--I have heard a female speaking in a foreign tongue--was about 2 years ago in a language unrecognizable to me--my father's family is Dutch--German--

The next day I sent a picture to Barb of Jane's grandfather. Again, I gave her no other information, just the picture. Here's what she wrote:

Wow, When I open this photo, That man's eyes went right through me. I felt like I was in trouble at school!
I want to say, "He was a nice man, had a good heart," but a voice keeps telling me, "not on the inside."
I feel like if you acted up, he would say, "get the strap" for you.
Wow, I am sorry...But I want to say nice things about him, but I just get creeped out.
He feels like a 'Professor', high end business man, someone with lots of habits & culture... "even if it's only in his head"! (That's the voice, not me.)
Had a son or brother, Cause it feels like that's the Male voice that is guiding me through his picture, I have to tell you he says, "No love lost".
OK, this is weird to me, when I ask him if he was 'married', I get a strong voice saying, "you need to ask?"
Is this hung over a mantle? cause he says, "I should be hung over the mantle."
Boy he really demanded respect.
Wow, this is up there with that other painting of the "Creepy boy"![A case we worked on that is written about in *Ghost Investigator Volume 10*]

Jane's response:

OMG--he Was hung over the mantle--My father got mad because I moved him to put Jenny Lind up there--when he married my grandmother he received a dowry of $50,000.00 and my father said it was a business transaction and soon had it spent--my grandmother left the house to my father and his 2 sisters---my grandfather talked them into selling it to him for about 3 or 400 dollars--he got my father's share for nothing promising *him the house when he died--he gave it to my aunt instead--He was the one with the rare book store and the parties--he left my grandmother and the children to fend for themselves up here while he lived in NY. They had a housekeeper Auntie Johnson---no relation to Alexander--- who raised the kids basically---when she became sick my grandfather told my father to dump her off at the closest poor farm--he was rotten according to my father.*

Obviously, the only thing better than having Barbara look at photos of the house was to have her visit the house, so we arranged to meet there on February 1, 2013. Barbara arrived first, and found a family member waiting for her—a deceased family member!

She described an older man sitting on the chair that was at the far end of the porch. The man was not happy with the placement of the chair, because he preferred sitting in the center of the porch. After going inside and introducing Jane and Rose to Barbara, our first question was whether they knew of any man who used to spend a lot of time on the porch.

"My father sat out on the porch all the time," Jane replied. "He would sit half way down and just watch. Especially in the summer, it was his 'sitting on the porch weather' he would say."

There was to be even more confirmation that Jane's father was still in the house.

Our first stop was the parlor, where Barb said, "You bring a lot of antiques in, things not from your family. And you bring things in with you."

She felt that a lot of spirits and energies were attached to these items, in particular, the couch. Barb kept "hearing the Lizzie Borden song" every time she looked at that couch and felt that something very bad happened on it, perhaps a murder? It was such a negative feeling that she wouldn't even touch it. Jane said that she has actually felt something grabbing her when she was sitting on that couch.

Then Barb started clenching and opening her hands and moving them in a very animated manner as she spoke, asking if Jane's father used to "talk with his hands."

"On my god!" Jane said, stunned. "That's exactly what he did with his hands when he spoke!"

13

Barb also sensed that her father had spent a lot of time in this room, and indeed, the parlor had become his bedroom at the end of his life. She later felt a sharp pain in her eye and head, "like an aneurism." Jane said the day her father died he grabbed his head and started screaming in pain. They didn't perform an autopsy, so she isn't sure whether or not it had been an aneurism, but it is quite possible.

We next went into the dining room where Barb sensed a little boy in brown knickers and a girl in a simple dress, about ages 8 and 9. They were mischievous and liked to hide things, the boy taking household items and the girl preferring jewelry. Jane related a story were an expensive ring was missing from the place where she knew she had placed it.

"I said out loud, 'Listen, I know that one of you took it. And I want it back right here on the desk when I get home in the morning.' In the morning when I got home from work it was right there on the desk where I had pointed."

As we were talking, Barb saw a man walk through the kitchen, describing him as being very tan, just like Jane's mother had described the man she saw. "He's a pain in the butt," Barb stated in her refreshingly blunt style. "And he comes from back there. [She pointed to the backyard.] Were there stables there? Like a barn worker in the old days?"

Jane couldn't think of anything at the time, but there would be an amazing validation later.

Rose and Barbara in the dining room.

We went into the kitchen where Barb sensed a sad older woman aching from her daily chores, and her days were very long. The woman had an accent, possibly Dutch or German, and she was responsible for cooking for many people, perhaps for "farmworkers or people arriving on stagecoaches."

Not connected with the kitchen, Barb then felt a child "who had been kicked in the head by a horse," possibly at a time before the house was built. We talked a little bit about the imprint that such tragic events can leave on a place, even when new houses are built on such a spot. In the paranormal world, as in real estate, it's all about location, location, location!

We went into the back room overlooking the yard, and Barb was certain there were several other buildings on the property long ago, and some of the activity in the house may be from spirits and energies from those structures. "And there were definitely horses," Barb stated again.

We then went upstairs to a bedroom that Barb immediately identified as having belonged to Jane's mother. Without going into personal details here, she was able to accurately describe both Jane's mother's physical and emotional condition. Barb also added that the woman was telling her, "I was a good healer."

"She was a nurse!" Jane confirmed. "And she was very proud of her profession."

I got chills at that point, realizing we had company at that very moment!

There was quickly even more company, as Barb asked about the woman who had a brother in World War I, which would have been Jane's grandmother. There was more discussion about family relationships in the past, which shed some light on what might be behind some of the lingering spirits. Let's just say it's rarely the happy and contented soul that stays behind.

Jane then showed us a photo of a baby her father had found stuck up in the back of a closet. He thought it might be a picture of Jane's

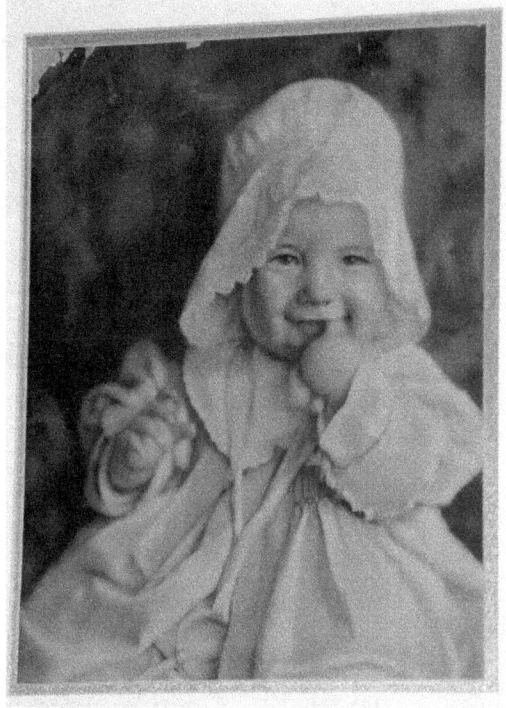

grandmother, but Barbara disagreed, as she felt something very different from the photo.

"You know there was a baby that passed on here," Barbara said.

"Oh, I knew it! I knew it!" Jane jumped in excitedly. "When I first saw it I got a creepy feeling. There was this young couple called the Easemans and they were only here for a very short time and moved out suddenly and sold the house to my grandmother. I always had the feeling that they left because they had a baby that died."

While it may or may not have been the Easeman's child, Barbara is convinced the baby in the photo died in infancy from some sort of lung disease or illness. She feels that the sound of a baby crying can be heard, and also felt that the child's silver rattle had been left behind. Jane does recall that her family found a silver rattle when they first moved in, and people have heard a baby crying!

Later, Barb said that Jane's mother kept saying the name Bobby, and at first, Jane said that there weren't any relatives named Robert. It was one of those blank moments I have seen during readings when people just can't connect the dots, even when they are very obvious dots. When Barbara kept repeating that Jane's mother was saying Bobby, light finally dawned.

"My father used to call my mother Bobby," Jane said. "Her name was Barbara and he just called her Bob or Bobby as a nickname."

In the attic, Barb encountered "a very stern man" who did not want us up there. "What are you doing in *my space*," she heard the man say "very loud and clear." She felt that the man, named Charles, had died in a house that was previously on the property. Jane confirmed that she and others "feel creepy" up in the attic, and there were those people who were pushed and felt threatened. Barb also felt that children were sent up here to punish them.

Then we went downstairs to the dining room where Jane showed Barb several family photos and pieces of jewelry. Barb held each one and basically read the family history from them, describing everyone's character—both strengths and faults—as if she had known them. During this time, a question kept coming to mind, but I waited for Jane and Barb to finish.

I had been trying to piece together all the things Barb had been saying about the woman feeding all the people like from a stagecoach, the child kicked by a horse, the creepy man who worked on the property with horses, and even when I first emailed her a photo of the house, she said something about there being a stagecoach stop. However, to this point, Jane didn't even seem to have knowledge of horses ever being kept on the property, but I felt the need to ask again.

"Was there a stage in this area? Was there a *Bloomingburg Stage* that would have been here?" I asked, emphasizing the name.

"*Oh my God!*" Jane suddenly exclaimed. "Now I remember! There was an old building in the backyard, and there was a sign on it that said *Bloomingburg Stage*. Can you believe that? That's so weird. I can't believe you said that!"

We all had a good laugh over the temporary amnesia, but it is certainly something we have seen, and all personally experienced, many times before. Unfortunately, the stagecoach building is long gone and the sign was given to a local historian, so hopefully it is still in good hands. But the fact remains, there was a stagecoach stop on the property, which brings a lot of the pieces of the puzzle together and makes more sense.

Will we ever be able to piece together the entire puzzle at the Emma Martin house? Probably not. There is so much that goes on within families—and in the hearts and minds of individuals—that it would be impossible to get the complete picture. But I think there is enough evidence to show that this is a house that carries the imprints and scars of the people who lived here, both good and bad, and in sickness and in health.

With someone like Jane living here now, someone who is open to the existence of many spirits and encouraging communication with them, this house presents a fascinating example of what happens when the worlds of the living and the dead meet.

If spirits want the attention of the living, they will certainly get it here. However, if some spirits are present to try to impose their will as they did in life, I doubt that's going to work out for them I the long run, as the more we learn about their motives and intentions, the less power they have over us. Hopefully, there will come a point where those spirits just give up and move on.

As I have often found, cases of hauntings have direct reflections on life, and I have often said that death does not improve one's personality. On the other end of the spectrum, I have also found that those who loved us in life stay with us after death. So this is a case where it is a mixed bag of spirits, with different agendas and "karmic baggage"—from family members, past residents and employees, to those who may have come in with the furniture. As beautiful as this house is, I don't know that I would want to live in such a place, but it certainly was an amazing place to visit!

Barbara in the attic.

To learn more about Barbara or to book a reading, go to:

Website: http://barbararothreadings.com

Email: barbararothreadings54@yahoo.com

The Overdue Spirits of the Nyack Library

The original library building from an early postcard.

One of the many things I love about librarians is when they give you a packet of information and photos regarding the history of the library and the haunted activity when you arrive to do an investigation!

In November of 2012, Mike Worden (http://paranormalpolice.com) and I—after having our customary pre-investigation buffet—went to the beautiful old stone library in Nyack, NY, at the invitation of the Children's Librarian, Aldona Pilmanis. This was not unfamiliar territory for me, as my father's family came to Nyack in the 1800s, and I would bet there were Zimmermanns who watched the library being built, and attended the grand opening in 1904.

The $15,000 structure was funded by a grant from Andrew Carnegie, hence his portrait that greets you at the main entrance, and throughout the 20th century the elegant library served the community. Of course, that community grew considerably, as did the function of the library, and expansions were completed in 1973, 1993, and 2010. Construction for this last addition began around 2006, and it was then that some strange activity began.

According to Aldona's wonderful reference, around the time of the start of that construction, "A nighttime custodian named Cesar claims to have been touched while cleaning book stacks in the old reference area. He was wide-eyed and freaked out when the morning staff arrived. He kept mumbling, 'Ghosts! You have ghosts!' He never returned to work."

Aldona wrote the following about what has occurred since that terrifying night:

- There are two claims in the Materials Management department (which used to be the old Children's Room). An employee saw the full-bodied apparition of a man in a small storage area with only one entrance. He looked at the man for about 2 seconds, registered what he was actually seeing, and turned and walked away. When he looked back, the man was gone.

- The other experience in the Materials Management department was when a full cart of books (very heavy) rolled towards an employee over the span of about three feet. The cart stopped just short of the side of his desk. He was alone at the time.

- The Director and two employees were on the upper floor after the library had closed, discussing the placement of shelving, when they heard footsteps coming from the café area. They called out to see if anyone was there and received no answer. One of the men walked over to the area, but no one was there. As he was walking away, the elevator dinged on that level (as if someone had called it). The doors opened and closed, but no one got on.

- A huge wall clock was found on the floor of the café area one morning. The clock was intact despite falling some distance, and the large pan head screw on which the clock rested, was still in the wall. The custodian was scratching his head about this one, as someone would have had to lift the clock up and off the screw. I personally reviewed the surveillance video and saw no one in the area for hours before and after the event—which happened at 10:51pm, a year ago in October.

- An employee whose office was in what is now the Director's office used to hear office doors (which no longer exist because of the reconfiguration of the building) open and close when he was alone in the building.

- About 6 months ago, I was in the cellar looking at the Children's items in the back portion of that area. I was completely alone and standing still. After being down there for about 5 minutes, I heard an EXTREMELY loud crashing sound that continued for about 20 seconds. I could have sworn we were having an earthquake! When the noise stopped, I went to where I thought the noise was coming from and discovered 10 sets of metal stand up shelving units in a jumbled heap. My guess is that they were stacked closely together and fell like dominoes—why, I don't know. When I made a comment to the custodian about the state of the shelves, he didn't know what I was talking about. Someone had righted them, but we cannot figure out who!

An impressive collection of activity for a place such as a library! Are past employees still going about their business amongst the books they loved? But what about knocking down the clock and the metal shelves? It's hard to imagine a former librarian would create such a racket!

As a concert had taken place in the library that night, we got a late start on the investigation. It was about 10:45pm by the time everyone (except Aldona) had left, and we decided to start with the café, as that was where the clock had come off the wall at 10:51pm. Quickly setting up our equipment, we sat with our eyes fixed on the clock. But alas, 10:51pm came and went without anything unusual happening.

However, several minutes later, I asked for a sign, and the right side of my face suddenly felt hot. Or more accurately, my skin didn't get hot, the air next to my face did. Mike and Aldona both felt the hot air, and we eliminated the heat vents 15 to 20 feet away as its source. This inexplicably hot air was just there about three to four feet from the floor in the middle of the café area. Mike went back to Aldona's office to get his thermometer, and even though several minutes passed before he returned, the area that had been hot still showed that it was several degrees warmer than the surrounding air.

As we were concentrating on this area, I was facing a section of books. I was saying something to Mike and suddenly stopped talking, as I was astonished by what immediately happened—a dark, shadowy figure went in front of a shelf of books and darted around behind them. I quickly glanced to my left to make sure a real person hadn't cast a shadow, and then I ran over to the book shelves. There was nothing.

I should clarify what I saw: it was an indistinct figure, and only visible from the waist up. There was no telling gender, clothing, or anything other than it was a dark, human shape—or at least half of one. And I have to be honest, as soon as I saw it I thought, somewhat disappointed, "It was only half a figure." I then quickly "heard" a possibly female voice say in a jovial manner, "Well, half a figure is better than none!"

Were the spices from our Chinese buffet enhancing my imagination, or had a playful female spirit just messed with me? I would swear in court I saw that figure, so I would have to go with the latter.

We checked the area with the EMF meters, and then Mike and I tried to recreate the shadow to be certain it hadn't been cast by any of us. To even get anything close to what I saw, Mike had to stand about 25 feet away from where we had been at the time of the sighting, and even then, it was a pale, faint shadow that did not have a human shape.

Aldona and Mike checking out the area where I saw the dark figure.

Unfortunately, even though we had two video cameras running, they had not been pointed toward the area where the shadow appeared. That section was just a few feet out of the frame, which was another disappointment. Of course after the fact, we aimed the camcorders towards those shelves. I even decided to sit on the spot where I saw the shadow, although as I stated at the time, "That has not always had the best consequences!" (I was thinking of such places as the suicide house I wrote about in *GI V7*, when I decided to sit on the suicide spot. Bad idea. Very bad.)

Nothing further occurred, but when I stood up from the spot, I noticed the section of books where I saw the figure was labeled "Visual Arts." Short of the "Paranormal" section, what better place for an apparition to manifest!

We then moved to the Director's Conference Room, which for lack of a better term, felt creepy. (Actually, that's the perfect term.) Our attention kept being drawn upward by noises in the attic, and we saw that the access to the attic was in the ceiling. After a considerable amount of time of hearing things we couldn't explain, Mike pulled down the ladder and, just at midnight, we ascended into a spacious attic with old wooden rafters. Stepping carefully, we moved around as much as we dared in the dark, unfamiliar surroundings.

Holding out my K2 meter, I asked if anyone was up there with us, and one light came on. I then asked if this person felt safe up there and all the lights lit up! At the same time, there were sounds up there with us we couldn't identify. The wind was blowing a fan blade in a vent, but that we could both see and hear. There were no signs of mice or squirrels, so we couldn't account for the sounds by blaming rodents. And I didn't know until we came down that the entire time we were up there, Mike had an intense pressure-type pain in his head.

What this all means I couldn't say, but my gut feel is that some spirit inhabits the attic, and its influence extends to the conference room below. And just for the record, I had one of those persistent thoughts that sometimes come during an investigation (that have often been validated later), so here it is—I kept hearing the word "twofold." I asked Aldona if it had any meaning concerning the library, and she couldn't think of any. But I know enough to throw those things out there at see if they stick to something another time.

Mike reacts to a strange noise in the Directors Conference Room.

Our next stop was the Materials Management department, where the member of the staff saw the man standing in a small storage room. Both Mike and Aldona felt uncomfortable in that room, but I didn't feel a thing. Where I felt "agitated" was in the computer area. We set up the equipment at both locations, but despite any feelings of creepiness, nothing showed up on audio or video. Unfortunately, the same was true for the large basement—plenty of atmosphere, but nothing in the way of evidence.

By this point, we were into the wee hours of the morning and we still had a long drive home. While we didn't get the physical evidence I had hoped for, it's not every day you see half of a shadowy figure dart by (remember, half a figure is better than none!) so I considered the investigation a success. Still, there were many mysteries in the library left to explore, so I knew we would have to return—and with our "secret weapon," psychic Barbara Bleitzhofer. The spirits can run from her, but they can't hide.

I returned with Barbara in February of 2013, and joining us that night were Aldona and her sister, Irena. As we were all very anxious to begin, we wasted no time starting the investigation.

Me, Aldona, and Barb.

The following are Barbara's impressions and the activity we all experienced that night.

Computer Room: "Very intense," stinging sensation in her arms. "*They* come down the stairs" into this area because they are drawn "to the energy" of all of the computers. She also felt that there is "a kid who runs around." She further explained that it's a teenaged boy "from that house"—she said, pointing to the Depew House across the parking lot, behind the library.

Barbara felt that it may have been a "sea captain's house" and added that "you can see her (that captain's wife) up there" in the cupola, worried and watching for him. I quickly said, "*You* can see her up there!" We both laughed, as Barb often gets so into it she forgets that others aren't seeing what she sees so clearly. Aldona confirmed that a sea captain did indeed live there.

Barb described more details about the family, and felt that the spirits from that house influence the library building.

"It just oozes energy," she concluded.

The Depew House.

Downstairs room where the figure of a man was seen and the heavy cart of books moved on its own: Barb's first reaction walking into this room was intense, and she immediately said, "Stuff moves around in here. Oh, Linda, who the hell *is* this guy?"

The male presence was not very welcoming to her at first, to say the least. She felt that he was a "take charge" kind of a man, and in an attempt to control things, he moves objects. He also thinks it's funny to touch and poke people.

"He's a bit of a trickster. He doesn't mean to hurt anybody, but he's a trickster."

She believes his name was Pete, and "he was only in his thirties or maybe forties" when he died of "consumption" and he "was related" to the Stevenson House next door.

I did a little research and found out the Depew House was built by Peter Depew, and his daughter Elsie married Dr. Stevenson, hence the name of house to the right of the library. Several descendants were

28

named Peter, so more research is necessary to see if any of them died of consumption.

We then noticed that one of the barcode readers—which is supposed to emit a steady green light—was blinking on and off. Barb asked Pete a series of questions, and the light appeared to respond. For example, she asked, "Pete, is that you playing games with us?" and the light went off. It remained off until she asked him to turn it back on!

At this point, Aldona was standing in the middle of the room, and Barb could see this man standing right next to her. Both of our K2 meters confirmed something was going on around Aldona as we got some very high readings, and just to her one side, not in front or behind.

Barbara also felt there may be someone named Richard, who was called Dick. There were other names as well, which was somewhat disconcerting as it suggested there were quite a few spirits out and about this area of the library.

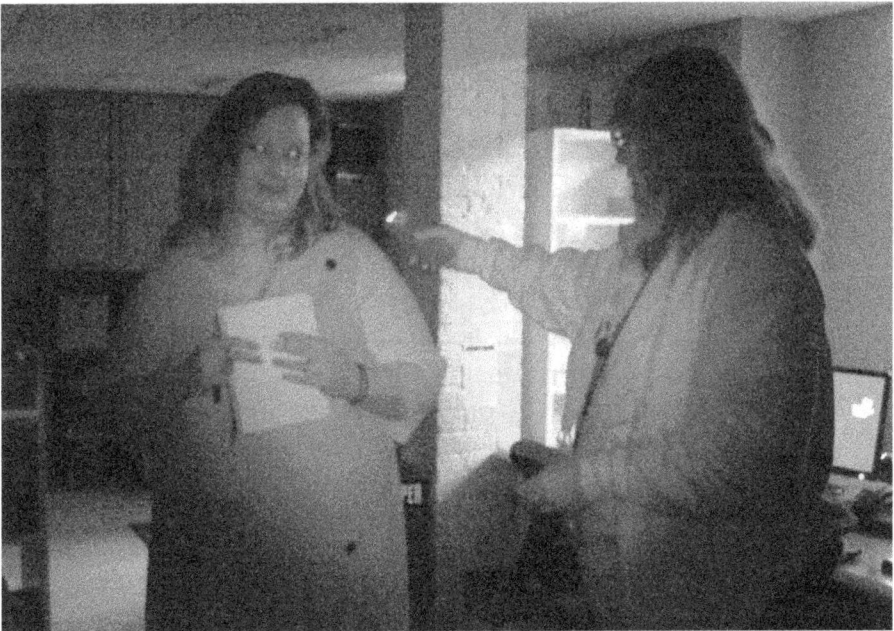

Barb checks out the EMF around Aldona. Note the K2 meter lit up.

Children's Area: We went into Aldona's office, and Barbara saw something "small and black" like a large cat or small dog move into a back corner. Aldona said that sounds in that corner often make her stop what she's doing and search that area, but she has never seen anything.

At this point, Irena stated that she was feeling "very emotional" and was concerned that something might be attaching itself to her. Barbara felt that she was sensitive enough to be picking up on the emotions of the woman who lived in the Depew House, both her worrying and the love she had for her husband.

As we approached the children's reading room, Barb stopped in front of the door and gasped and said it was very intense. Aldona responded, 'Oh no, this is our happy place." That remained to be seen.

We went inside and my ears starting ringing and buzzing. I felt like a wave hit me, and I stammered, "Wow, what's wrong with the…what's going—I didn't feel this last time here."

Then one of the most amazing things to ever happen to me on any investigation—or anywhere else—hit me like a ton of bricks.

"You know, it's funny," Barbara said, looking and pointing right at me. "I'm hearing that old time song, *Will the circle be unbroken, by and by Lord—*"

"Oh no, no, no!" I practically shouted, cutting off her singing. "They just sang that at Bob's mother's funeral!"

"Get the heck out!" Barbara replied, as stunned as I was. "That's all I keep hearing over and over."

"I just got totally covered in goose bumps," I told everyone, rubbing my arms as I spoke, and then got all choked up.

I managed to explain that just a week earlier at the funeral service of my mother-in-law, they only played one song—*Can the Circle Be Unbroken* by the Carter Family. Everyone was standing holding hands during the song, and Bob and his three sisters were standing by the casket together. It was obviously an extremely emotional moment and one none of us will forget. I personally was not familiar with the song, but it had been very meaningful to Bob's mom and dad. Now, it's a song I will certainly never forget.

As I was admittedly totally "freaked out" at that point, Barbara waited a couple of days to tell me the rest of the message when I

30

wasn't so upset. She later told me that a woman had come to her as that line of the song played over and over in her head. That woman wanted Barb to say to me that I would understand what it all meant.

What it meant was that my mother-in-law was there in spirit at her own funeral and knew exactly what was going on. It meant that she knew she could reach me through Barb that night. It meant that since I do what I do with the spirit world, she knew I would understand that it was her way to let me know that she was okay. And I'm sure she also knew that I would tell Bob and his sisters about this incredible message, as it would bring them some comfort.

It still gives me goose bumps just thinking about it, and when I listened to it all again from my digital recording of the night, it just gave me chills. The spirit world works in mysterious and amazing ways!

We continued on as I tried to refocus, and Barbara concluded that there are a lot of outside influences at work in the library from the buildings around it. Why is the Nyack Library acting like a magnet for the spirit world? Barbara feels that this land used to be a place where people would meet, picnic, play, etc., and it still attracts a lot of activity.

We left the story room and went into the main book stacks. We heard a loud, close banging or knocking sound, as Barbara was seeing a young boy sitting on a shelf. She said he was from the Depew House, and that he "enjoyed the dancing." I immediately wondered what dancing could possibly have to do with a library.

"We dance here [with the children] all the time!" Aldona said. "We always do the Hokey Pokey."

Who knew?

Carnegie Room: "Massive chills," Irena commented when we first walked in.

Barbara's hand quickly went to her throat and she asked if anyone had died here, possibly when the original building was being constructed, or from an earlier building. Her voice was uneven as she spoke, as if she was having trouble breathing. The picture that emerged was of a workman who got caught up in a rope, fell from something high, like scaffolding, and had his neck broken or was strangled to death.

She also saw "four that linger here," referring to four men. "Was there another building here, possibly a barn? There must have been, and these men were connected to it."

I later searched photo archives at the library, and found a photo from 1890 of the Depew/Stevenson barn that once stood on the property!

Top Floor and Director's Conference Room: As we were going upstairs, both Barb and I heard "the rustling of skirts," footsteps, and a noise back by some book shelves. Aldona reminded me that those shelves were where I had seen the half of a dark figure when Mike and I were there the first time.

Barb went over to that area and started getting a metallic taste in her mouth, which I didn't understand. She explained it "was not good," and it was something that happened when in the presence of a negative entity. She felt that this was the man she sensed in the Carnegie room, the one who died in the accidental hanging

As Aldona related the incident with the clock coming off the wall in the adjacent cafe, we all heard—and recorded—a loud banging sound nearby. Barb felt that this same unhappy spirit was responsible for taking the clock off the wall.

As we went toward the Director's conference room, we heard some popping or clicking sounds. Aldona said she believed it was just the heating system, but then there was a very loud bang. We all looked at one another and simultaneously said, "That was not the heat!" We had heard many sounds that night, but that one was so loud and so close it really sent chills up our spines.

There were some more amazing revelations about current and past employees—either still living or with family members in the area—so I will not divulge those details, but it all went to bolster Barb's assertion that the energies of the people who worked here are strong.

Shortly after when we tried to leave a secure area, even though Aldona entered the proper code and the green light came on, the alarm went off. This happened several times—the code was accepted, the all-clear green light came on, but the alarm would sound. We joked that someone didn't want us to leave, but had it lasted much longer it wouldn't have been funny!

Another Section: We then went into another section of the library and I have to keep this confidential, but Barbara tapped into the energy of a another former employee, and according to Aldona, described this person exactly, even mentioning the exact gift the staff gave this person. It was like she was reading a biography of this person's life, career, and present health. Out of courtesy to this person, who is still alive, I can't say more than that, but believe me, it was an incredible display of Barb's abilities.

I should also point out, that at other times during the night, Barbara accurately described the personalities of the various staff members when we passed by their desks or offices. I pointed out that I had never seen her pick up on the "living people" so much. She replied that she feels that energies of both the living and the dead are held and amplified and held in this building.

Basement: Our next stop was the basement, which was accessed via the elevator. As we approached, Barb said that the "someone" rides that elevator, so it looks like it goes up and down on its own—which Aldona confirmed does happen.

Once in the basement, Barb and Irena both looked physically affected by the heaviness and intensity of the atmosphere.

"I don't like this place," Barb stated. "It's like they hide from you, waiting to catch you off guard. It's like they would even throw boxes or something at you."

That certainly rang a big bell, as Aldona had that terrifying encounter where all the shelves had been knocked over when she was alone in the basement. We went over to the spot where Aldona had been standing when the shelves began "falling like dominos." Barbara immediately said, "It was the man in the derby hat," as if she was clearly seeing him at that moment. In fact, at that moment, she had seen a man in a derby hat "peering around the shelf," and we all froze.

Just then there was a very loud sound from one of the furnaces turning on, which startled all of us—some more than others. Barb gasped and slapped Irena's arm in surprise. It certainly broke the tension and we all laughed. Especially when Barb joked, "Girlfriend, you do not want to go on a ghost hunt with me because you will come out bruised!"

It was an amusing end to our investigation, just what we needed after hours of intense concentration and intense activity. In the following weeks and months, Aldona kept us informed of any new encounters, and sent us the following:

• Just found out that we had another sighting of an apparition at the library yesterday morning around 8:30 am. A coworker was standing at his desk in the Materials Management office (the area where Barbara sensed the man Peter), when he saw someone walk across the room. He thought it was a staff member and said "Hey Jim," but got no answer. No one was there!

• Just wanted to report that we had a sighting of "Peter" yesterday. If you will recall, he is the one that Barbara picked up on in the Materials Management section that used to be the old Children's Room and was the one that was standing next to me while we were investigating there. Anyway, he was spotted yesterday by Matthew (the employee who originally saw him the first time) but this time it was in the cellar. Matthew said that he was rushing through the aisle, and looked to the left when he reached the end. He said Peter was just standing there. Like last time, Matthew said that he was gone in an instant, but the interaction was long enough for Matthew to realize that it was the same entity he had seen ages ago. Pretty cool! Still hoping that one of these days I will have a sighting of my own here!

So, what are we to make of the Nyack Library and its many, many spirits? To begin with, this is a place that for some reason retains the energies of the people and events on this land before the building was constructed. It also holds on to the energies of past and present employees, like some paranormal card catalogue of everything that takes place here. For those who are sensitive, this makes for a potent mix which may manifest as full-bodied apparitions, be felt as emotions or physical sensations, or be seen and heard loud and clear, such as in the case of the falling shelves.

Libraries have always been some of my favorite places; islands of great knowledge in a world often swimming in ignorance. While I had certainly visited other haunted libraries, I never experienced one this…well let's say, "noisy" with ghosts. Is the land, the stones, the books, or something else we can't even fathom that draws them all here? We can only guess.

Just remember, the next time you want to read a book about ghosts, try reading it in the Nyack Library—a place writing its own history of the paranormal.

The library takes on an eerie appearance in the dark.

Body of Light

In early 2013, I received an email from a man who had an experience he couldn't fathom. I agreed to keep his identity anonymous. The following is in his own words.

I lived in Monsey [NY] a few years ago while doing religious Jewish studies. In religious practice, some men go to a ritualistic bath everyday called a Mikva. The Mikva is considered to wash away some degree of spiritual uncleanliness which has affected the body as well. Women do this also after menstruation. Men typically go in the morning, during the day. Anyway, one day I had missed going in the morning and decided to go late at night, about 11:30pm, after bowling with a friend. It was the summer so my friend sat outside the house with his windows down. While waiting, he kept his car running with the headlights on, which were bright up against the side of the house 1 foot in front of his car. I went inside the house, which was a religious high school with a Mikva in a section of the building. I couldn't find the light switch in the dark so I propped the door open. After dunking in the Mikva water, I was standing at the shower to rinse off. I was warming the water up with my head looking sideways. In the passage of light which spread through the small room from the hallway outside the propped door, I saw a person walk by me very quickly. His body was covered in light. From my side view, not the "corner of my eye" it was obviously a person. I assumed it was my friend coming in. I started talking to him. When there was no response I looked in the corner of the room where the figure walked into a few feet from me. There was no one there. I felt terrified, being 100% certain someone walked next to me and who I saw as what I would call a body of light. I threw on my jeans, grabbed my underwear, shoes and other belongings and ran outside nearly naked. When I got to our car the windows were closed, the headlights were off, and doors were locked. I banged on the door to open up quickly. When I got in, my friend was equally frightened and nearly hysterical. We kept cutting each other off trying to explain what happened. He related that while he was sitting in the car, windows down, headlights bright against the wall of the house, that right in front of the car he saw a person, a body of light, run in front of the headlights. It sounded identical to what I saw inside. He was so frightened he closed the windows and locked the doors. We kept telling over the details and drove home all shaken up. When we got back we told friends but they sort of chuckled. It was impossible to tell anyone with any degree of seriousness. When I bring it up today with my friend who experienced this with me he also chuckles and says, "yeah that was freaky." Not much to say, and in fact it's awkward to talk about.

Some months later my Rabbi's son showed me a book he bought called, "The Ghosts of Rockland County." It was your book so I always kept you in mind as someone I could tell my story to with some seriousness. Even now I don't believe my own experience. It was so out of my worldview and common understanding that it becomes conflicting to consider it. And of course I feel crazy telling anyone, but it was unforgettable and real.

In a follow-up email he wrote:

I want to add that the event has left me with a bothersome question which is, why did I experience this and what did this body of light (or whatever it was. I don't know how to describe it) want with me or the space I was in?

I wish I had an answer for him!

Proprietary House

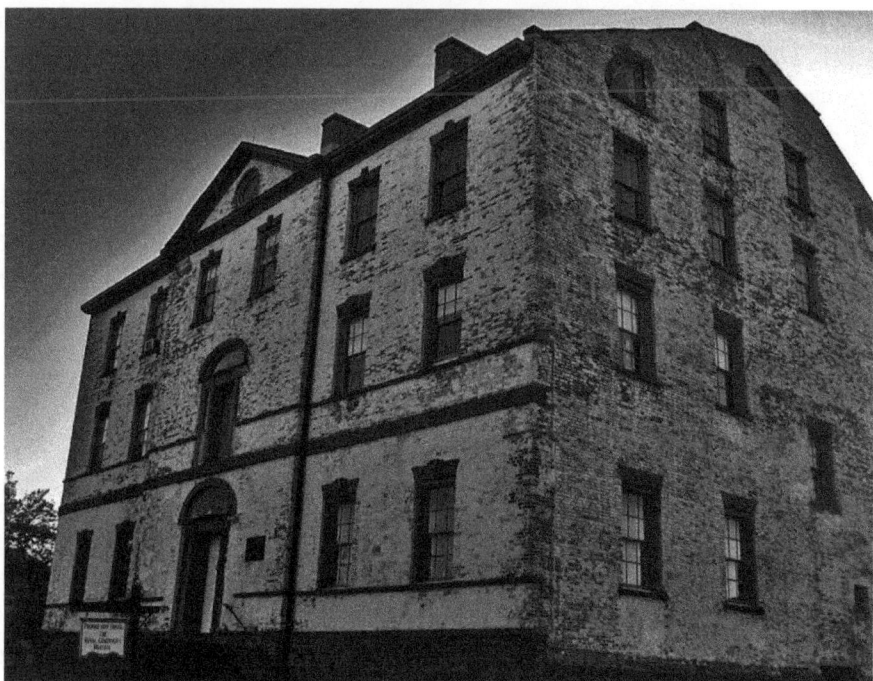

This case came to me from an interesting source. In 1998 when I decided to write my first ghost book, *Ghosts of Rockland County*, I didn't know what to do about a cover. At one of my astronomy lectures in New Jersey, I met Gordon Bond, who was a graphic artist, and also happened to work at a printing shop. I can't quite recall how it all fell into place, but Gordon became the cover artist for my first ghost book, as well as several more of my books over the years. And all the while, he was a skeptic when it came to the question of ghosts.

Fast forward 15 years, and Gordon is still a skeptic, but also an historian and published author, and the On-Site Coordinator of the historic Proprietary House in Perth Amboy, New Jersey—a very haunted building, if other staff members and visitors over the years are to be believed. In April of 2013 while arranging for me to come down to give a ghost lecture during the Halloween season, Gordon asked if I would like to come down sooner to check out the place and conduct an investigation. He didn't have to ask twice. It took a couple of weeks to coordinate schedules, but on May 4 we were all able to get together.

Of course, police detective Michael Worden and psychic Barbara Bleitzhofer would be joining me, but we also had a new member of our team—Felix Olivieri of Big Guy Media. I first met Felix when Barbara and I were on the first episode of his show *Paranormal Valley*. He also produced and directed the feature length film based on my UFO book, *In the Night Sky*, which won the People's Choice Award at the International UFO Congress in Arizona in March of 2013. Felix had been to many haunted sites to film his *Paranormal Valley* shows, but he had never been to a place just to investigate, and he never had any experiences of his own—until this night.

We all met at my house to drive down to Perth Amboy together, and naturally I had made some brownies for the road. It was a fun-filled trip, and we all laughed and talked about all kinds of things, except the Proprietary House, as we didn't want Barb to know anything about it so she would go in with a blank slate. But let me fill in that blank slate for you readers.

Perth Amboy was settled in 1684 because it was an excellent port for shipping and quickly became an important center for government in the Colonies, as well. According to the Proprietary House website:

> Between 1674 and 1702, governance of the British colony of New Jersey was divided into the two political entities of East and West Jersey. Each was under control of a Board of Proprietors, wealthy landowners who leased and subdivided their properties. The East Jersey Proprietors chose Perth Amboy as their capital, while West Jersey selected Burlington. In 1702, governing power was turned over to the crown, though the Proprietors remained an influential real estate corporation. The Royal Governors that followed would split their time between Perth Amboy and Burlington, renting lodgings and local spaces in which to conduct government business.

As royal governors deserved a royal residence, plans for a suitable mansion were set in place.

On March 25, 1761, the Board of the Proprietors of the Eastern Division of New Jersey (to give them their full title) proposed to construct a fine mansion worthy of serving as the residence of the Royal Governors. They hired the architect John Edward Pryor to design and build what they called the "Proprietary House." This was Pryor's first commission in America, though he would go on to design and oversee construction of a number of important buildings in colonial New Jersey and New York. He arrived from England on July 14, 1761 and was able to record in his accounts book for April 3rd of the following year: "Set the labourers to digging."

The original structure consisted of four levels. In the basement was a kitchen, wine cellar, servants' hall, butler's quarters, and housekeeper's room. The main floor encompassed an entrance hall, drawing room, governor's study, dining room, study, breakfast parlor, and housekeeper's quarters. Upstairs was the master bedroom, dressing room, and guest bedroom. Tucked under the eaves were more servants' quarters. Sixteen fireplaces warmed it in winter and it could boast such advanced architectural features as lead gutters and the protection of a lightning rod.

It was a magnificent structure to house the representative of the King, the Royal Governor himself, but it didn't serve in that capacity for too very long, thanks to a little thing known as the Revolutionary War. However, the one governor who did live there had a rather well-known name—Franklin. The Royal Governor was none other than William Franklin, the son of Benjamin Franklin. One can only imagine the friction between the famous Founding Father and his staunchly loyalist offspring! There is an account of a fierce argument witnessed between father and son during one of Ben Franklin's visits to the Proprietary House, but William would not disavow his allegiance to the crown.

That loyalty led to William's arrest in 1776, and imprisonment in Connecticut. William was released in a prisoner exchange in 1778, and eventually moved to England. Ben and William would only meet again on one occasion, and they would never reconcile their differences.

The fate of the mansion hung in the balance when it was gutted by fire in 1784. Fortunately, it was restored by John Rattoon, who had been a British spy during the war, acting as a go-between for Benedict Arnold and Major Andre.

William Franklin

Rattoon was so good at his craft no one knew he was a spy until the 1900s.

The next owner, Richard Woodhull, expanded the structure and in 1810, opened the luxurious Brighton Hotel. The War of 1812 didn't help business, and in 1817, the property was sold to Matthias Bruen, who turned the mansion back into a private estate.

Bruen died in 1846, and the former royal residence would undergo even more changes:

> Following Bruen's death, his heirs resurrected the Brighton, attracting wealthy guests, including military officers during the Mexican War and Civil War. Nevertheless, another downturn in the economy forced it to close and by 1883 the Bruen family conveyed the property to the Presbyterian Board of Relief for Disabled Ministers and the Wives and Orphans of Deceased Ministers, who called it The Westminster for the next twenty years, before returning it to the Bruens. In the early 1900s, the land was subdivided and the once great lawn cut down by Kearny Avenue. It was sold to J.P. Holm who operated it as the Westminster Hotel in the 1920s. The mid-20th century saw the building's decline into a run-down boarding house with rumors of prostitution. Fortunately, however, local residents remembered its place in history and would come to its rescue.

Help was slow to materialize in the last half of the 20th century, even though the Proprietary House was the only original remaining Royal Governor's mansion left in the country. Finally, groups were formed, donations were raised, the state got involved, and the building's restoration began—a process still ongoing.

Something else is also ongoing—the haunted activity that can be experienced anywhere at any time. Members of the staff have reported footsteps, voices, a small boy in 19th century clothing, a woman in white, and a very dark, shadowy male figure. People have been physically touched, there have been inexplicable lights, and my favorite—the police asked the staff to please remove the female manikin standing in front of a window, as they keep thinking someone has broken in after hours. The only problem is they don't have any manikins in the house!

When we arrived, we were greeted by Gordon and his wife, Stephanie, who does historic conservation. We brought all of our gear into Gordon's office and decided to do a walkthrough before another group of investigators joined us.

I should first point out that Barbara had called me earlier in the day to ask if the place we were going had ever had a murder, or a murder-suicide, as she was already getting impressions. I didn't know the complete story of the mansion, so I told her I didn't know, and then stored that in the back of my mind. She also said that somebody "very, very famous had been there," and I just replied, "Maybe." Again, I wanted her to know as little as possible about the place.

Our first stop was the kitchen in the basement, which now serves as the gift shop. Barb's immediate impression was that there was a stern woman who wanted to know what we were doing in her kitchen. She also asked if there was ever some sort of a bar or tavern in the place, and Gordon told her it was a hotel for a period. She also felt a nervous man who anxiously watched everyone.

"Did you know there was a fire?" Barb asked Gordon.

"The place burned after the American Revolution," Gordon said.

"Okay, that counts," I concluded smiling, happy to see that Barb was on target once again.

After some discussion about a general in riding boots Barbara saw, she asked if they had found things larger than musket balls, but smaller than cannon balls. Later on, we went into a room with display cases, and there were just the objects she had described. She also felt that someone had received a sharp blow to the head. At this point, Felix turned because he thought he saw someone walking behind him. Mike also thought he saw something moving.

All this and we hadn't even gotten past the first room!

One of the display cases with some of the artifacts found on the property.

We went into the tea room, which was definitely unlike any tea room I had ever been in before. It was an arched, brick construction with no windows, and reminded me of more of a powder magazine in a fort than a place to sip Earl Grey and nibble on scones! Gordon explained that this was the first room to be constructed, and at various times over the centuries the room had been used as a wine cellar or for food storage, and a restaurant, but Barb felt that a "lot of people were huddled in here," as if hiding or afraid of something. Unfortunately, there's nothing in the historical record to shed light on that.

The unique tearoom.

We then headed upstairs to the drawing room, and Barb immediately sensed "dancing, with a punch table." She felt it was a joyful place that had seen many parties and special occasions. I pointed to the portrait of William Franklin over the mantel, and without telling her who he was, I asked what she felt.

"Fear. Fear, and very strong-headed, strong-willed about things," she said. Taking a deep breath, she added, "He seems like a little man, too, like a Napoleon syndrome type of person."

Gordon didn't know how tall William Franklin was, and I have since been unable to find a physical description. Then Barb asked something very interesting—whether the man in the portrait was the son of the person who built the house or owned it at one time. We replied that wasn't the case, but I asked her why she referred to him as "the son."

"It's almost like daddy would have been not that proud, because he didn't do certain things certain ways," she replied immediately, clearly sensing the conflict between the patriot father and loyalist son.

I said that what she was saying was interesting, but still didn't tell her who the man in the portrait was, in case any other information came through. We then moved on to the impressive entrance hall and main doorway. It was here that Barbara first mentioned hearing "a lot of kids running around." Of course, that can happen in any household, but I recalled that this place had once operated as a home for widows and orphans.

When we went into the dining room, Barb said that there must have been a writer there. Gordon joked that we had "two right here," referring to himself and me. Then I pointed to Mike (author of *Ghost Detective*) and corrected him that there were three of us. Of course, that's not what Barb meant, and she went on to explain that someone tried to chronicle the history of the place, in a kind of romanticized way. Hopefully, we will be able to uncover the identity of this writer someday.

Barbara, Gordon, Stephanie, Felix, and Mike in the front entrance hall.

She then mentioned that at least two children had passed in the house, as she could hear them crying. I immediately noticed a surprised look of Felix's face, and he said, "That's weird, because I was just thinking about a crying baby."

Felix went on to explain that for a while he had been hearing kids both laughing in a group, and one crying separately. What was even stranger, was that he was hearing it clearly in an ear in which he is partially deaf! He also said that at several times he looked around because he heard a cat meowing. There were no cats or kids in the house—none that we could see, at least!

A moment later, both Felix and Mike looked up and asked if anyone else had just heard that baby crying. I didn't hear anything, but they both agreed that it sounded just like a baby crying upstairs. (Mike and Barbara also commented on the sounds of children laughing or running through the house at various times.)

"And I'm the one who never senses anything!" Felix added.

"I know, you're Mr. Skeptic," I said, amused

Felix telling us what he was hearing.

that the nonbeliever was having such dramatic and clear experiences.

Felix told Gordon that before filming one of his shows, he would always go to the allegedly haunted site the day before to plan the setup of all the equipment.

"So I spent a lot of time alone in places that were supposed to have a lot of haunted activity, and I never felt anything," Felix said, clearly not expecting to be having these experiences.

46

We went into the formal dining room, and Barbara said she didn't like the feeling in there, "because there was a lot of loud discussions in here, *a lot of turmoil*. Not just discussions, turmoil, like fights. I feel that they were more like big shots, you know, discussing and arguing in here, what was going on out there. They were arguing about *the state of what was going on out there*."

Could she have been picking up on the fierce arguments between Ben Franklin and his son about the fate of America?

As the upper floors are filled with rented offices, we were unable to go into any of those rooms. However, on the staircase Barbara "saw" a purple doorway, which was good, but also red patches, which she had never seen before and felt signified danger. She also said something about a "jumper," feeling as though someone may have jumped or been pushed out a window on an upper floor. We would find out the significance of that later.

We gathered in the drawing room for a little quiet EVP session. There were several noises, but with the proximity to the street and other houses, it was difficult to say if something was banging on the floor above us, or someone had slammed a car door nearby.

Barbara talked about someone there who sailed on clipper ships and dealt in spices. As Perth Amboy was an important harbor, this is certainly possible.

I kept hearing the word "providence" in my head, over and over again—but not the city, I felt it was more of an emphatic "*It was providence,*" type of impression, as if someone had truly believed that fate had played a role in an important event. I could really picture a man pounding his fist on a table, arguing with someone, "That it is divine providence, don't you see that?" While the impression was steady and persistent, I couldn't tell to what it was specifically referring.

Mike pointed out that the phrase "divine Providence" was used in the Declaration of Independence. Was I tapping into a tape loop of the past from the days of the Revolution, that famous confrontation between Ben Franklin and his son, or from the days that this place was a retired ministers home?

While this was going on, Felix was again hearing a cat or kitten meowing.

I also heard a noise down the end of the hallway near the staircase, so I decided to go sit by the staircase alone and see what happened. To me, this spot felt icy cold and was the creepiest place in the building. I kept looking up as if expecting to see a man leaning over looking down. I also had the strangest and most unpleasant feeling that someone who was regularly drunk or drugged would lean over that banister to throw up. That was a new sensation from the paranormal realm! Unfortunately—or perhaps fortunately—I didn't get too much time there as the other team of investigators arrived.

Greg Caggiano, a Trustee and historian who conducts some of the house tours, has also conducted numerous ghost investigations in the building, so he had valuable information about the history of the place in terms of both the normal and paranormal. He was accompanied by Kevin Finucan, Jake Reid, and Steven Allegretta. (And they also brought pizza, which to a bunch of people who had skipped dinner was a most welcome addition!)

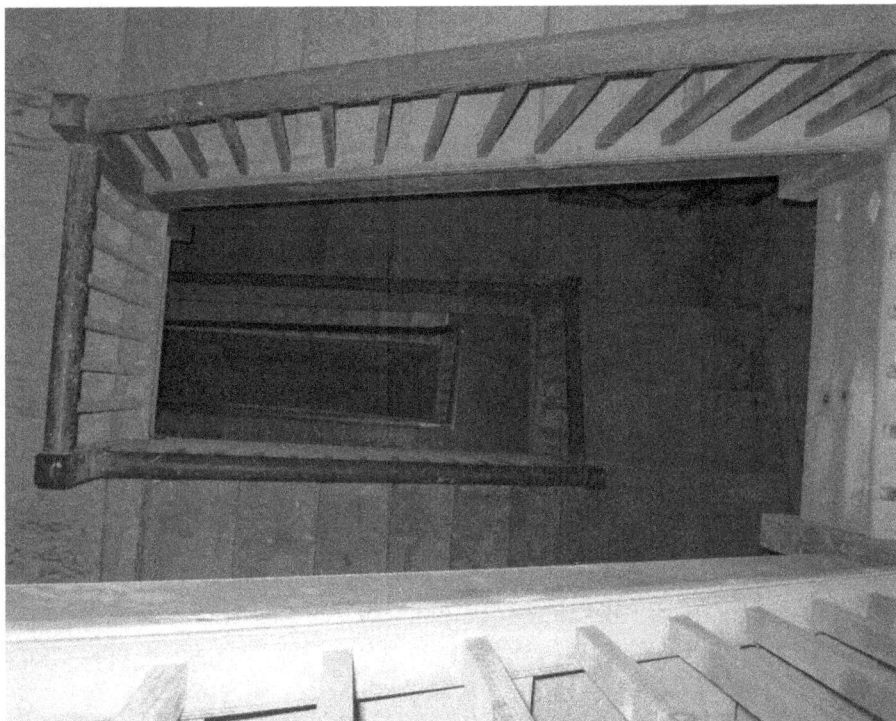

In my opinion, the staircase was the creepiest part of the building.

After they brought in all of their gear, we began a second walkthrough. Starting at the staircase, Barb described the purple and red colors she had seen. Greg had nothing to add about all the red, but he said a previous member of their team, who was a psychic, had also talked about seeing purple in the same area!

Greg asked Barbara—who still didn't know any of the history of the house other than it was both a private residence and a hotel—if she had any sense of any other purpose the house had served. I don't think he had even finished his sentence when Barb blurted out, "Whore house."

Greg kind of laughed at the instantaneous response, but confirmed that yes, indeed, this was a house of prostitution during WWII. He also added, "That part is not on the tour."

Barb asked about a murder-suicide, and Greg didn't know about any, but did say there was one documented murder. In the 1800s, a boy's uncle pushed him out of an upstairs window! That was exactly what Barb had said, that someone fell from a third floor window to his death!

This murdered boy has often been seen, usually dressed in blue. Visitors at special events have asked about the authentic-looking child reenactor, but there has never been a child reeanctor present on these occasions.

We went into the dining room where Barb told Greg about all the arguing she sensed that went on there, but he was looking for something very specific. He asked her to stand in one corner of the room, where she hadn't stood before, and asked if she felt anything. Her first impression was "a really nasty taste" in her mouth, as if someone didn't have the best dental hygiene, or any at all.

"And I feel like I'm going back and forth like I'm getting drunk," she quickly added. "That feeling that you can't stand up. He was very drunk."

"You win the prize!" Greg said, obviously impressed with Barbara's abilities.

He went on to say that when the place was a boarding house, this little section of the room was walled off into the caretaker's apartment. (Greg later told us that all the magnificent rooms in this mansion had been subdivided into tiny apartments.) This caretaker was a one-armed alcoholic who used to roll his own cigarettes using very strong pipe tobacco. He was found dead in his chair at that very spot, and still had a half-smoked cigarette in one hand, and a bottle of Jack Daniels in the other! Greg said that other people have felt a drunken wave sweep over them in that spot. What a shame that a feeling of a drunken death is the legacy that this man left to the world!

We asked about any cats in the house, and Greg said that people have seen a "ghost cat." Felix talked to Greg about the meowing he had heard several times, and it was probably good to know he was not the only one to hear the phantom kitty. Greg also said that two years ago someone had held a séance in the building, and every participant had felt a cat rub up against their legs! And someone else had seen a cat in an office just the week before.

Greg asked about another part of the dining room where a psychic has claimed there was some type of energy field or, that ever-popular and overused term, a vortex. None of us felt anything, and then Felix spotted something significant. By following the lines of the ceiling, walls, and floor, he astutely picked up on the fact the there's a significant curvature and dip in the structure at that very spot.

No one had ever noticed that before, but it made perfect sense that if you are walking along and all of a sudden the wall and ceiling in front of you are curved and there's a depression in the floor, there would be a sudden sensory shift that something had changed. In a house with a reputation for being haunted, that feeling could easily be misconstrued as being a paranormal energy field. Instead of warped space-time, however, it's clearly just warped wood. Score one big debunking point for Felix!

Greg also mentioned an incident that occurred recently. He heard the "thunderous laughter" of children in the hallway, and fully expected to find that some kids had broken in and were playing and fighting just around the corner. However, when he turned the corner the sounds stopped and no one was there. The sounds of children laughing and playing were also something heard by Felix, Mike, and Barbara.

We went back into the drawing room, and Greg mentioned something about Mrs. Franklin. I said that since the Franklin name was now out of the bag, we could tell Barbara all about William living there and his conflict with Ben. It was good to see those final pieces of the puzzle fitting together in Barb's mind to complete the picture of all the things she had been sensing about famous people, a father-son conflict, and men arguing about the state of affairs in the country.

Mike's attention is drawn to something, or someone, on the staircase.

We continued the investigation in various parts of the house, with Greg describing numerous apparitions that had been spotted over the years, and of other inexplicable occurrences. Specifically, there's an unpleasant and potentially dangerous spirit they call Byron on the main staircase; and in the tea room, several people have heard and felt a French woman. I was beginning to think I needed a score card to keep track of all the various spirits in this place!

In that tea room we finally had one of the EMF meters light up when we asked Greg about other activity there. It went off again when Barb was talking about sensing the people crammed in there and huddling together. Unfortunately, despite the EMF readings, there's nothing in the historical record to indicate it was ever used as some type of shelter or prison.

Across the hall is the servant's dining room, and this time when we entered it felt completely different. I found myself pacing back and forth in a somewhat agitated manner. I also sensed a woman who was not happy we were there. When Greg asked about the character of the woman, I immediately responded, "Bible thumper," and a heartbeat later Barb was saying the same thing! She also added that this agitated woman was always preaching to people. I wanted to spend more time in this room, but Greg wanted to show us a room we hadn't been in before.

Gordon, Stephanie, Felix, me, and Mike discussing the activity in the building.
Photo courtesy of Barbara Bleitzhofer.

There was a cramped utility room in the basement where Barb sensed a "not nice man." As I stood listening to Greg tell us that this tiny space with the furnace and pipes had also been an apartment in the 1950s, the door swung inward and hit my camera. No one was close enough to the heavy door to give it a push. It didn't appear to be unbalanced and we were unable to reproduce the door moving on its own. It wasn't hard enough to be threatening, but it certainly got my attention.

We then went back to the servant's dining area to further investigate the self-righteous female spirit. Mike and I got our K2 EMF meters out and I was drawn to a corner that had a spinning wheel. As I was asking, "Are you in the corner?" the meter lit up and a chill swept through me. I was startled by the sudden intensity and said, "Whoa! Did you see that?"

"Are you here now?" Mike asked, and the meter lit up again.

"Yes she is!" I exclaimed. "Why are you here? Do you want to tell people *the word*?"

Again, as if in direct response the meter lit up. This was truly remarkable!

I then told this woman it was time for her to go, although it felt like she was determined to remain deeply entrenched in this house. We asked a lot more questions, but after I told her it was time for her to leave, we got no more than a flicker on the meter. However, I continued to feel very "adversarial" and agitated.

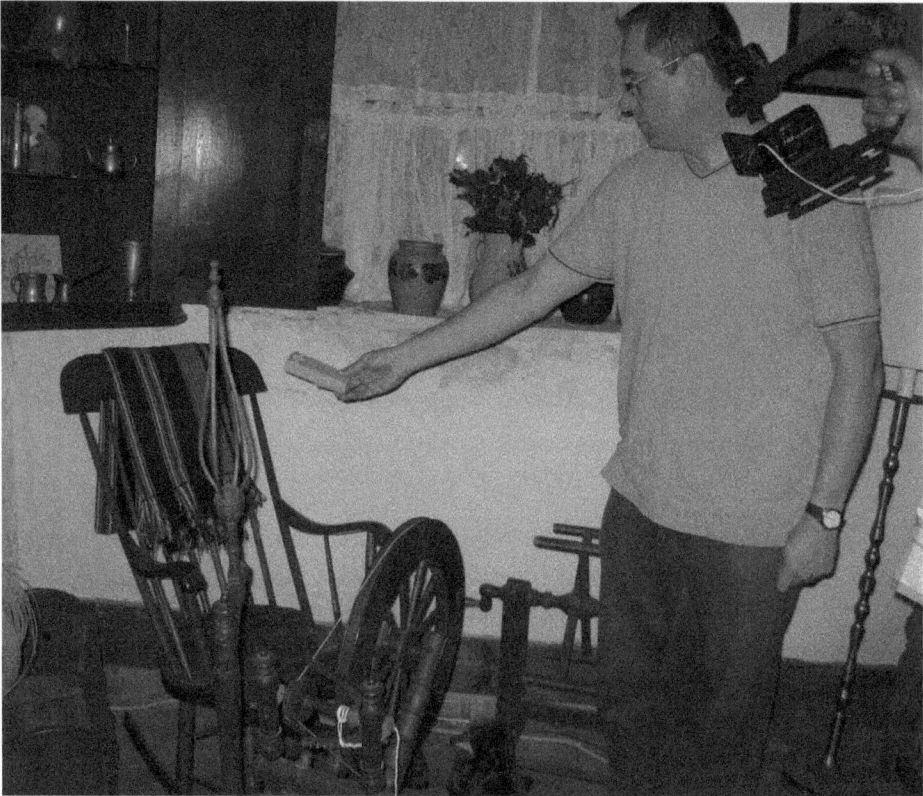

Mike by the spinning wheel where we got the very high EMF
readings and the distinct impressions of the agitated spirit.

We would have loved to explore more of this place, but everyone had a long drive home, so we reluctantly started packing our gear. I'm sure that even as amazing as all of our experiences were that night, we had only scratched the surface of the activity. As much as we may have wanted, you can't expect over two and a half centuries of human drama to all manifest in one night!

Even with just that one night, however, the Proprietary House made it onto my personal list of favorite haunts. Between its colonial roots and Ben Franklin connection, to its darker side of crimes and tragedies, this is what keeps ghost investigators motivated! And best of all, it's a place where you, the reader, can explore the paranormal world up close and personal. Just remember, in the world of ghosts, as in life, be careful what you ask for!

For ghost tours, history tours, high teas, and special events, go to:
http://www.theproprietaryhouse.org

Barbara captured an intense moment in the dark with this
flash photo of Felix hearing something inexplicable.

The Light That Never Goes Out

Even as a child, Leslie Weinberg always had very vivid dreams—dreams of things that would often come true. She also had an uncanny sense about people, and her first impressions were always spot on, too. She just assumed everyone else had the same abilities.

Leslie, Norman, and their daughters.

Unfortunately, one of those feelings she had was that her husband, Norman, would die young; a feeling that Norman also shared. Then about 14 years ago, came the day he was diagnosed with a brain tumor, and he was given 3 months to live. Those three months stretched into almost nine years, but still, Norman did die young. And it was right after his passing that things *really* got strange.

During his eulogy, the lights began to flicker and the microphone started making strange sounds. Someone light-heartedly suggested that Norman (who had been an electrical and cable TV contractor) was letting everyone know he was with them. Everyone laughed, but the inexplicable electrical anomalies continued in many different locations—especially lights flickering—and they still occur to this day.

For example, a friend of one of Leslie's daughters told her that he was communicating with Norman's spirit. She didn't believe him, so she put out this challenge, "Norm, if you are here, give me a sign so I know it's you."

Suddenly, a light bulb burst!

One day a cousin suggested that Leslie come for a visit to cheer her up. There was a treacherous section of road she would have to travel to get there, and a storm was coming, but she decided to go anyway, and brought an overnight bag in case the weather prevented her from leaving. In fact, the storm prevented her from ever arriving.

The water on that hazardous road caused her car to hydroplane, and the vehicle spun out and flipped over. As the car was going out of control, Leslie heard a voice—Norm's voice—telling her, "Les, it's not your time."

The damage to the car was so severe that the highly experienced insurance adjustor had been certain that whoever was driving had been killed, yet Leslie walked away with barely a scratch. Had Norman protected her?

Little signs of Norman's presence continued, even when Leslie was in Italy with a friend. The light in their hotel started flickering, but her friend refused to believe it was anything paranormal so she called maintenance. They could find nothing wrong with the bulb or the lamp.

When Leslie finally decided to start dating again, she used online sites to find compatible men. One of her rules was that any prospective man had to live nearby. She broke that rule when she came across a widower named Gary Heitman. She just had 'one of her feelings', and it turned out, as she later discovered, so did he.

There was definitely some chemistry between them, but there were also sparks. On one of their dates, they started having an argument in the car. Suddenly the radio turned itself on, and the lines that were being sung were, "I know you wanna leave me, But I refuse to let you go," from the song *Ain't Too Proud To Beg* by The Temptations. Not only was this type of music her favorite, but the words made her stop and think how foolish the argument had been. She felt it was Norman giving her a sign.

"Okay Norm, I get it," Leslie said. "You can stop it now."

Even though Gary didn't believe that Leslie's deceased husband was giving her signs and causing electrical disturbances, he decided to continue dating her—much to all her friends' surprise! But Gary was to have his own experiences soon enough.

Leslie and Gary

They were in Gary's house (which had belonged to his parents) and had just gone to bed, when Leslie looked up toward the ceiling and thought she saw a light. Then there was another, and another, "like a little meteor shower." The room also seemed to fill up with smoke, and "the little flecks of light congealed, dissipated, and came apart again." There was also a shape, almost like "translucent butterfly wings." Was she dreaming?

"Gary, do you see that?" she whispered.

"You mean the lights and the smoke?" he replied, obviously seeing the same bizarre phenomena.

At first Leslie was terrified, but after a while she felt it wasn't threatening and "decided to just watch the show." She also decided to raise her hand and see if she could touch whatever it was.

"It was like smoke was coming out of my hand, and when I moved my hand, the entire thing moved. It was like being under a pond and watching the ripples spread out."

What or who was this sparkling, rippling energy? When Leslie looked over to Gary, she saw an image of a fedora with a feather in it. Later, Gary took his father's fedora out of the closet and it was identical to the one she had seen! So was this energy the spirit of Gary's father?

Perhaps, but they have both seen this sparkling, smoky energy in several different locations, including hotel rooms, *but only when they are together*.

Leslie and Gary sent me some photos of themselves and family members for me to show to Barbara and see what she could sense. The one thing that kept coming through loud and clear was that Norman was still with Leslie. Apparently, even after death there is one light that never goes out.

There Are No Coincidences

This is another of those "coincidence cases" that "just happened" to come my way. It was a nice Saturday in August of 2013, and my husband, Bob Strong, and I were out running some errands. We decided to make a detour for a garage sale on Orange Turnpike in Monroe, NY. As I was walking up the driveway and saw this magnificent house, my Ghost Investigator senses started to tingle and I said to Bob, "If only I could get into this house!"

As I was going through all the antiques, books, and craft supplies in row upon row of boxes covering the driveway, I heard Bob talking to the owners as if he knew them, which it turns out he did! In fact, it was Nancy and Dale Forsberg, and he had gone to high school with them in Rockland County!

Okay, so I already know it's a small, strange world, but it got even stranger. It turned out, they had sent me an email years ago about activity in their house, but we never followed up to arrange an investigation. But now here I was, and I wasn't going to allow this opportunity to slip by, so we set a date for the following Wednesday.

And one more curious thing: The 1814 main portion of the house was built by the same builders as McGarrah's Inn and Masonic Lodge in Monroe, which is also haunted! You can read about my investigations there in *Ghost Investigator Volume 6*.

In any event, Nancy and Dale didn't plan on moving from their place in Rockland County, NY. Dale had been commuting to Washingtonville for 25 years, and they were both happy in their home. Then one day at work in November of 1995, Nancy got a real estate flyer in the mail that advertised a beautiful old house in Monroe. She loved it, but unfortunately, the price was not pretty, so she threw the flyer in the garbage.

Dale rarely stopped by where Nancy worked, but this day he decided to drop in. He asked what was new, and for some reason Nancy pulled the flyer out of the garbage and showed him the house. Even though the price was beyond their means, they decided to take a look. And what was not to love with this house and property?

The original 18x18 cabin/house was built before the Revolutionary War, and then was added to several times over the generations, until it became over 3,000 sq. feet of elegance and charm. And with over 2.5 acres of land and a couple of barns, the possibilities were endless. But there was the small matter of that big price.

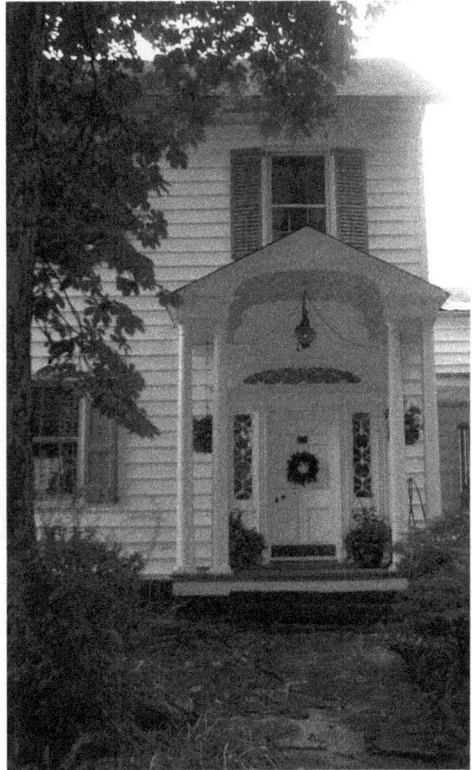

Then came January 31, their wedding anniversary, and as Dale was leaving for work, Nancy told him to "Be careful."

"He had been driving the same commute for 25 years, and I never said to be careful before."

Unfortunately, as if it had been some sort of premonition, she was correct. On Route 6, Dale hit a patch of ice—and so did all of the other motorists—and his car "was accordianed" in a multi-car accident. Fortunately, he was unhurt, but something snapped that day.

"I've had it!" Dale told Nancy when he got home.

He didn't want to do that commute anymore, and they decided to see what they could do about moving into the beautiful and historic house in Monroe, which was just 10 minutes from where Dale worked.

"We had to beg, borrow, and steal," Nancy said laughing, "but we got the house."

A friend made this beautiful painting of their home.

Before moving in, Nancy asked the previous owner if they ever saw any ghosts here.

"He acted like he didn't even hear my question. Then my brother-in-law also asked about ghosts, and again he just ignored the question."

They later found out why from a neighbor: Yes, the owners had experienced things, including seeing a woman in white. They most likely didn't want to jeopardize the sale of the house by admitting it was haunted.

Are any of these women from the family who used to live here the "Woman in White," or is she from an earlier time?

Nancy's first inkling that something was up, was when she was sitting on the front porch with a neighbor, Donna McGuire, a teacher, who also happened to be a psychic medium. She told Donna that this place was so beautiful that she and Dale didn't know how they ended up here, as they hadn't been looking to move.

"I know how," Donna said, in a matter-of-fact way. "The spirits of this house *chose you*."

Donna was later to surprise Nancy even more when she told her a series of names. Not only did all the names belong to Gignoux family members, who lived in the house in the 18th and 19th centuries, but they were siblings who had scratched their names into a bedroom window on December 28, 1886!

As we were to find out, there were also other names on that window, and one very prominent date: August 28—the day of our investigation! That date also happens to be the birth date of the Forsberg's son, as well as several other significant events. Just another coincidence?

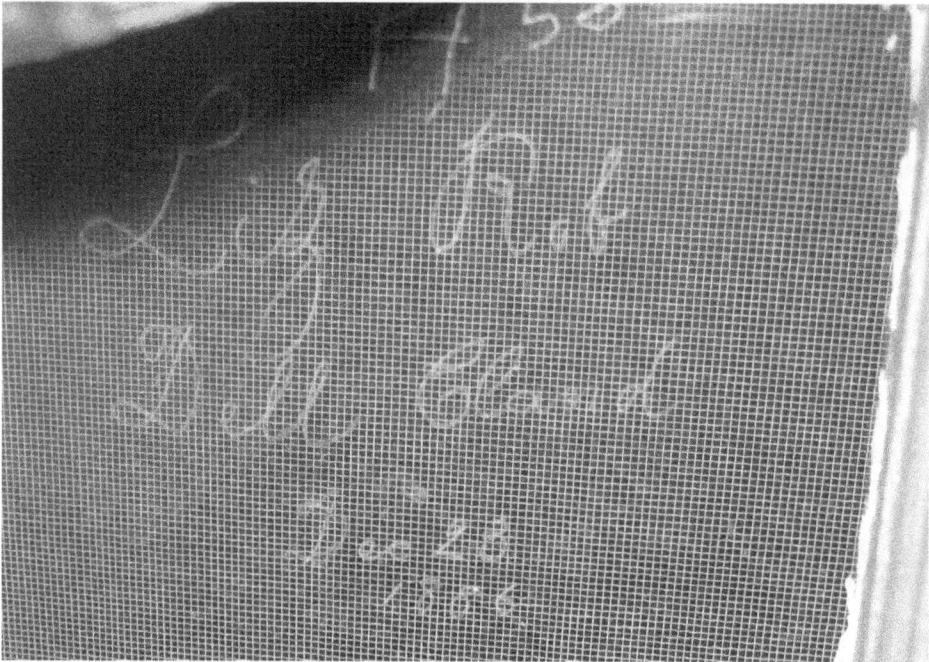

Siblings Liz (Elizabeth), Rob (Robert), Dell (Adele), and Claud scratched their names into this window on Dec 28, 1886. The date of August 28 was near the bottom of the window in even larger letters, but the photograph of that inscription didn't come out very well.

And speaking of the history of the house, while nothing is known about the 18th century builders or residents, it was Robert Fowler—first supervisor of Monroe—who had the large, 1814 structure built for his 16-year-old bride, Elizabeth Galloway. Robert and Elizabeth had no children, but after he died, Elizabeth remarried and started a long line of Elizabeths that lasted until 1955.

An old photo of the property. Note that Orange Turnpike is a dirt road.
Below is a close up of the house and some children.

One historical fact that the family apparently tried to downplay, was that they had owned slaves. No one is quite sure where on the property the slave quarters once stood, but it's likely that somewhere near the house there is also a slave burial ground. The Gignouxs were also initially buried here, but for some reason, they were all disinterred and reburied by the Methodist Church in Highland Falls.

Nancy has gathered scrapbooks full of the documents, letters, and photos pertaining to the house and the people who lived here, so she has been an excellent caretaker for history of the property. And now she and Dale are part of that history, in more ways than one.

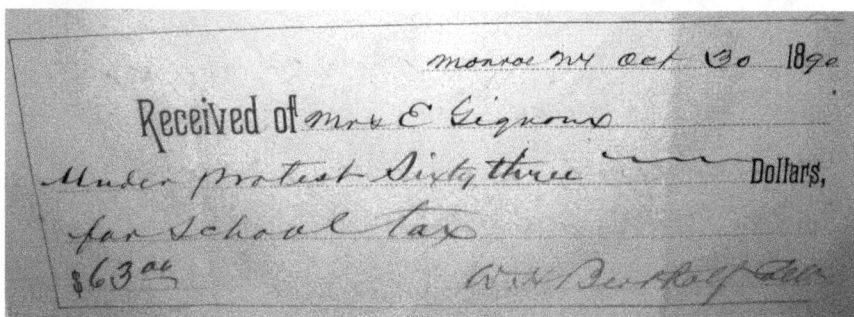

In 1890, Elizabeth Gignoux paid the $63 school tax "under protest." Don't we all!

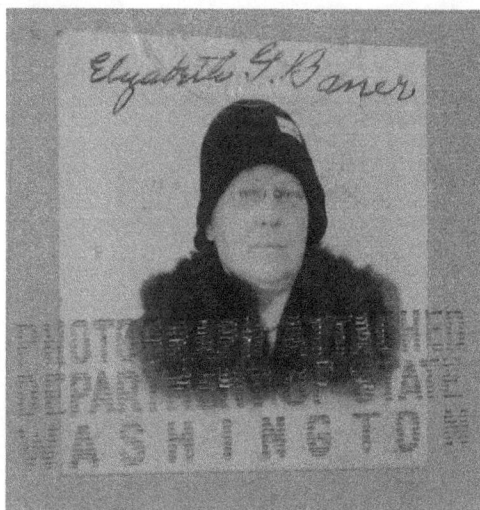

The 1932 passport photo of Elizabeth Gignoux Baner.

When they finally found out that the previous owner had seen a woman in white, they decided not to tell their 17-year-old daughter, but she found out anyway—the hard way. One night when she was in her bedroom on the second floor, a woman in a white dress appeared in her doorway. They later discovered that years ago someone else had also seen this woman in white standing by a fireplace (below) in the oldest section of the house.

In addition to this mysterious apparition, books have suddenly "jumped" off of shelves, a music box started playing on its own, other objects have moved without human hands, and they have smelled cigarette and cigar smoke. One evening when Dale was in bed, he heard footsteps approach the bedroom (below), the hinges creaked as the door opened, and a female voice whispered his name—and it wasn't Nancy or his daughter! Also, at different times, both Nancy and his daughter heard their names being whispered.

An infrared image of one of the bedrooms.

At first, they were all reluctant to share their individual experiences, as they thought the other family members would think they were crazy, but finally someone mentioned an experience, and then the truth came spilling out—this house has ghosts!

After listening to the many stories, we toured the house. I felt like I should have brought breadcrumbs so I could find my way back, as it seemed like a maze of rooms, hallways, and stairs. Couple that with some low, slanted ceilings and low doorframes, and I was starting to get the sense of walking through a funhouse—a paranormal funhouse.

I do have to mention, though, that even though I felt that we were not alone, nothing ever seemed threatening or ominous. Even the basement was "decidedly un-creepy" as I put it, despite its old, dark recesses and cobwebs. If there are ghost here—and I'm fairly certain there are—they are friendly, or at least benign. Of course, seeing a white apparition of a woman or having your name whispered may be scary or unnerving, but I don't think anyone or anything here means any harm.

Bob has to bend down to clear the low ceiling on the attic stairs.

And speaking of unnerving—after the tour, everyone went back to the kitchen, but I decided to have a little "alone time" and EVP session in the room where the woman was seen by the fireplace. I didn't have to wait long. I started my digital recorder, said what time it was and where I was in the house, and *just 9 seconds later* I clearly heard footsteps coming down the hall toward the room I was in.

I don't know why, but when I turned, I expected to see Donna in the doorway. I must have interpreted the footsteps as being from a woman. But there was no Donna in the doorway, no Nancy, no anyone. I jumped up and ran into the hall. No one was there, either. Still on the run, I went back to the kitchen and asked if anyone had gone into the hall, but no one had left the kitchen. I had to conclude that whoever was walking down the hall toward me was not a living person.

I believe my reaction upon realizing that was, "Oh, cool!"

As there conveniently was a psychic medium in the house, I decided to see what—or more correctly, who—I had stirred up. Donna joined me in the parlor adjoining the same hallway where I heard the footsteps, and she did feel as if quite a few spirits quickly gathered. I had hoped to get some insight into who they were and why they were still here, but they apparently had some other topic of discussion in mind—me!

Donna began by saying they were all excited about the number 11, and wondered if that meant anything to me. I told her that I was working on *Ghost Investigator Volume 11*, and that this story would appear in that book. She said that made the spirits happy.

Of course, always having my skeptic shields up when meeting a new psychic, I realized that anyone going to my website would know I was working on Volume 11. But then Donna and the spirits delivered a slam dunk. In fact, several slam dunks that just amazed me.

For example, she put her hand to her mouth and asked if I was having any problems with my teeth, or if I planned on going to the dentist soon. I was having some slight, occasional discomfort with a back molar, but didn't have any plans of going to the dentist about it, especially since the dentist I had since I was a child had just recently retired, and I hadn't yet chosen a new one. Well, 36 hours later, a piece of that tooth broke off, and I had to scramble to find a new dentist.

Lucky guess, or coincidence, you might say? Well, get this:

Donna said that the spirits were giving her a name that sounded like Lowry or Lori, but it was spelled Lawry or Lawrie. I recorded her trying to say this name, as she slowly and carefully sounded out each syllable and the different variations. I remained a calm observer throughout all this, even though I easily could have fallen off the couch because I was so surprised.

And what earth-shattering and deeply spiritual connection did this have to me? Was it a long lost relative or dearly departed loved one? No, it was a baseball player, and one that was very much alive. Allow me to explain.

I am a huge baseball fan—HUGE—and have been since I was born. I'm a New York Mets fan to be exact, which has probably gone far towards my ability to empathize with suffering spirits, but I digress. I also naturally happen to be a NY Yankee hater—a third generation Yankee hater—so between innings of a Mets game, I'll switch to the Yankees in hopes of seeing them lose.

The night before the ghost investigation, I turned on the Yankees-Blue Jays game, and the announcers were saying what sounded like Brett Lori was coming up to bat. When I saw his uniform, I saw that his name was spelled Lawrie. So there I was, all alone, talking to myself saying, "That shouldn't be pronounced Lori. It should be Law-Ree or Lar-ee." And so it went, me saying out loud the various possible pronunciations of the name.

Fast forward 24 hours, and there's Donna surrounded by the spirits of this historic house, who somehow knew exactly what I had said in the privacy of my own home! How that all works I don't know, and maybe I don't want to know, given the complete lack of privacy we appear to have from the spirit world!

Donna went on to tell me many other personal things that no one else could possibly have known, but not a single thing about the spirits themselves! It was a crazy mixture of fascination and frustration. Yes, it was very cool—and kind of creepy—that the other side knew what I was doing the day before, and what would happen two days later—but could they have taken a moment or two to identify themselves, maybe give me a date or two, or anything of historical significance?

Everyone then came in the parlor and we all spoke for quite a while, but it started getting late, so I packed up my gear. But even as we were leaving there was a little paranormal parting gift. When Bob and I opened the doors to the van, the interior lights didn't go on. That had never happened before. We tried opening and closing the doors a few times, started the van to make sure the battery wasn't dead and that we still had headlights, and then finally went home.

The next morning, Bob found that a switch on the dashboard must have been pushed to turn off the interior lights. The switch was not in a location that you could push it accidentally, and the interior lights had been on when we arrived. Somehow, the button was pushed while the van was locked and we were in the house!

From left to right: Donna McGuire, Dale Forsberg, and Nancy Forsberg.
To contact Donna for a reading, email her at: djqm@optonline.net

I definitely plan on returning to this house for a more complete investigation—if the Forsbergs are still living there, that is. The house is currently for sale, and at the moment a doctor from New York City is interested. That would certainly be fitting, as two previous owners were doctors with practices in New York City. Perhaps the spirits are already working behind the scenes choosing who *they want* to be the new owners?

A hand-hewn beam in the attic.

Note: I wrote this story on the Thursday and Friday following the investigation. On Friday, a plumber was working in our basement, as I worked on the story in my office. I had just finished when I heard him calling me, so I went down to the basement to see his work, and pay the bill. As we were talking there was a loud "thud" from somewhere upstairs. We looked at each other, and he asked if I had heard it, which of course, I had.

Then there was an even louder sound. I asked if there somehow could have been air that had gotten into the pipes. "Not like that!" he replied, clearly concerned. Seconds later we heard yet another sound, like someone moving around, and he became so concerned he insisted on coming upstairs with me as he was sure someone was in the house. We cautiously went upstairs, but all the doors were locked, and no one else was there. After he left, I said out loud that no spirits were allowed to follow me home, and should go back to where they came from.

I hope they did.

And I wonder if the plumber will ever return.

Infrared image of me checking EMF in the attic.
Below, the view down the staircase.

The Factories

Back in 2001 and 2002, I was working on a massive project—the writing and editing of *Rockland County: Century of History*. I think I traveled over every square inch of the county during my research, and took many photographs for the book. One of the more memorable sites I visited was the collection of old factory buildings in Garnerville, NY.

Two things in particular stood out about these long brick buildings and alleys—they looked like something out of 19th century England, and they kind of gave me the creeps! Who knew that more than a decade later I would be back, and this time I would be researching the haunted history of the place.

The opportunity would come through Hallie Coletta and Gary Tribert, high school friends of my husband, Bob. (Just as the Forsbergs were in the previous chapter!) Hallie is a very talented and successful graphic artist and set designer who has worked on countless Broadway plays and television shows. She has a studio in one of the buildings, and was actually the one who painted the Garnerville Arts and Industrial Center logo on the side of one of the buildings.

Hallie painted the front of her studio wall (yes, that's just a flat wall!)
and the logo on the outside of a building.

Gary is a lifelong musician who has played in bands since the 1960s. He used to have a studio in another building where his band practiced, often late into the night. Between Hallie and Gary, they had some very interesting stories to tell.

First, however, I need to tell the story of this site.

In the 1700s, a grist mill was built along the Minisceongo Creek. In the 1820s and 30s, the Garner brothers replaced the mill with a calico printing factory. The business grew and in 1853 became incorporated as the Rockland Print Works, "for the purpose of manufacturing, printing and dying woolen, cotton or linen goods." Over the decades it continued to expand to become one of the largest companies in the country, and boasted such perks as Christmas bonuses for employees. The company also built a YMCA, the S. W. Johnson Fire Company, and basically owned the Village of Garnerville, maintaining "the streets, lights them from its own power plant, and polices them."

Unfortunately, the Depression hit the business hard and many of the buildings were abandoned. Down, but not out, a new owner formed the Garnerville Holding Company and began renting space to various businesses. That practice continues today under the direction of Robin Rosenberg, current president of the company. And while manufacturing still takes place, the arts have also found a home here.

Perhaps a ghost or two has also found a home, which is why Bob and I met with Hallie and Gary in August of 2013. Of course, every ghost has its own story to tell, and that story often involves a tragedy. It is safe to say that 19th century factories were decidedly unsafe places to work, and many accidents must have occurred, some of which proved fatal.

For example, while searching through newspaper archives, I came across this article from the *Haverstraw Messenger*, dated December 3, 1869:

On Tuesday of this week, Alexander Davidson (uncle of the Superintendent of the Rockland Print Works), while attending to a vat of boiling dye stuff, accidentally fell in and was horribly scalded. As soon as he was able to get out, he plunged into a vat of cold water, which only prolonged his suffering. He lingered in the utmost agony for about twelve hours, when he expired.

What an awful way to go! And he wasn't the only one to die a horrible death. In September of 1875, a terrible fire swept through the factory's buildings:

At a recent fire in Haverstraw, N.Y., two-thirds of the Rockland Print Works were destroyed by fire, viz: The old dye-house, starch-room, plaiting down room, wash-room, and steam chest room, and the large engine of eighty-horse power. The roof of the packing house was also burned, but no damage was done to the goods. Some unfinished goods were burned. The exact loss is not known. There is full insurance. Peter J. Dennan, foreman of the printing room, was killed instantly. Dennan and several others were on a bridge connecting the printing building with the wash house, when the gable wall of the wash house fell, breaking through the roof of the bridge and the pin-sticking room. Two others were severely injured and two others slightly hurt. The estimated loss ranges from $225,000 to $330,000.

I find it remarkable that this article goes through all the damage in detail and makes sure to mention it was all insured, before it bothers to mention the crushing death of one of the employees! I also found another article about the fire which stated that two people were killed, so perhaps one of those severely injured didn't survive. I also found a brief article about another fire that occurred in 1871.

When Barbara Bleitzhofer looked at the photos I had emailed her of the factory buildings, this was part of her response:

"Feels like I can't breathe due to smoke. It keeps making my eyes burn. Was there a fire in there? My hands hurt from it."

Apparently, these tragedies have left a lasting imprint.

Of course, not all deaths were so violent. With close to a thousand people working there at any given time, natural deaths were also bound to occur:

September 4, 1895, *Stricken at His Work, Sudden Death of Mr. Hodson at Garnerville: Richard Hodson, an engraver at the Rockland Print Works, Garnerville, was suddenly stricken with apoplexy* [usually a cerebral hemorrhage or stroke] *at 3 o'clock yesterday afternoon, while at his work...Mr. Hodson was 38 years of age and leaves a wife and seven children. He was apparently in robust health up to three o'clock yesterday, when he was suddenly stricken down.*

The doctor arrived to try to save Mr. Hodson, but he was dead before they could get him home. (And now that I read this again, maybe it wasn't so natural a death! Only 38 and in "robust health" up to the minute he died of some sort of apoplexy!? Sounds fishy to me.)

In more recent decades, there are records of a woman's body found on the property, and there was a young man was shot and killed by police after committing a robbery.

While waiting for Gary to arrive, Hallie took us on a tour of the streets, alleys, and tunnels of the complex. The sun was beginning to set, casting eerie and unnerving shadows. As I ducked down alleyways to get photos, that creepy feeling I experienced years ago returned. I told Bob that all this place needed was some fog and Jack the Ripper, and it could be the streets of Whitechapel in London in 1888.

When we went into the building that contains Hallie's studio, I was amazed by the unbelievably long hallways, and the remnants of the past, like the huge mechanism that used to power the elevator. One could only imagine what conditions were like when these factories were in full production—the heat, the cold, the constant din of the machines, and the long, long hours of work.

Gary soon joined us, and our first stop was a building where there is a large carpentry shop. The owner of that business told Gary that he sees "*them* all the time in here"; shadowy figures that walk about the enormous room. We quickly started getting some EMF readings at various spots around the room. My attention kept getting drawn to a large doorway at the back of the room, and unless my eyes were playing tricks on me, I thought I saw something moving past that doorway. I went back there to another enormous room and sat quietly for a while, but nothing else happened.

One of the long, eerie, hallways.

Hallie had some sort of ghost radar app on her iPad—and I have to say I am highly skeptical of such apps—and this one occasionally produced a word. One of the words was "rope." Of course, we had no idea what that meant, if anything. But a short time later, Hallie, Bob, and I were in a long storage room and I came across the biggest pile of rope I've ever seen.

Still not taking the situation seriously, I said that perhaps this was the rope the spirit had mentioned on her iPad, and with that, my EMF meter lit up and Hallie and I both felt "an intense presence" that made us woozy and somewhat disoriented for a few moments. There were plenty of goose bumps to go around as we stood in the darkness of the old factory by this huge pile of rope.

The EMF readings faded, until I asked if this rope had any significance, and again the meter lit up. A few days later, I sent a picture of the rope to Barbara, with no information, and she sent back the following:

"Ok, that is the first time that "Ropes" made my head spin. Too many people met deaths here, by the rope! I keep hearing that. Some "people" walk in there due NOT to working deaths, but by the hand of others. Jealous workers?"

Then she added:

"Fights, from both sides. I keep hearing the song, "Both Sides Now." I feel like I'm in the 1800s when the Irish workers had to fight for their rights. Linda, I also want to keep putting my hands up to fight.

"Dizzy from it. Very loud place. I hear, 'Don't talk, work,' but they still talk. Oh, this place is wild. They follow you around here. Holy smokes, this place is very active."

One other thing Barbara mentioned was that she pictured "a small rock/brick room with people in it, down below, almost like a jail cell. Not a good place to be put." Hallie later told me that Robin said there were catacombs under the factory buildings. Were those underground rooms used for punishment? Unfortunately, we didn't know about them at the time, but I guarantee that if given access, I'll be down there on the next investigation!

Hallie, Gary, and Bob check the high EMF readings in the carpentry shop.

We then went to the building where Gary used to have his studio. He told me that on three or four separate occasions, he would open the studio and find that the snare drum had been unhooked and removed from its stand and placed on the floor upside down. He couldn't understand why any of the band members would come back after he locked up the day before and do this with the drum. When he finally asked who was doing it, no one had any more of a clue than he did!

Flash photo in the dark of Gary and Bob is Gary's old music studio.

Another time Gary was in the studio practicing by himself, and left for lunch. When he came back, a framed picture that had been on a bookshelf in the corner was smashed in the middle of the room. There had been things piled up in front of that picture, so there was no way it could have even fallen off the shelf, let alone end up in the middle of the room.

Gary couldn't understand what was happening, until one night when they were all practicing rather late. Their drummer, who had been Peter Frampton's drummer, suddenly stopped and looked wide-eyed and white. Gary asked what was wrong.

"Didn't you see that!?" he replied, obviously stunned by something he had just witnessed.

The drummer went on to describe a Civil War soldier who walked right out of the wall as if it wasn't there, continued across the floor, and disappeared through the other wall! These walls were all put here in relatively recent times, so during the Civil War, this would have been wide open space. Perhaps this soldier still sees the place as he knew it? And, perhaps this soldier had been a drummer, which is why he kept removing the snare drum, and made himself visible to a fellow drummer?

We sat for quite a while in that room, but alas, no soldiers walked through, and apart from some sporadic EMF readings, nothing happened. We sat in the dark and talked for a while about some of the other feelings and experiences associated with this site, and it all made it abundantly clear that this was a location that would require several investigations.

I considered this night a "scouting expedition" to get an idea of the scope of the place and its ghostly activity. We only had access to three buildings that night, but between the stories, the history, and my personal experiences I was very grateful to have the opportunity to get into such an amazing place.

What more is there to discover lurking down all these dark alleys and in dusty corners? Stay tuned, as I have only just begun to investigate!

For more information:
Garnerville Arts &
Industrial Center
55 West Railroad Avenue
Garnerville, N.Y. 10923
www.garnervillearts.com

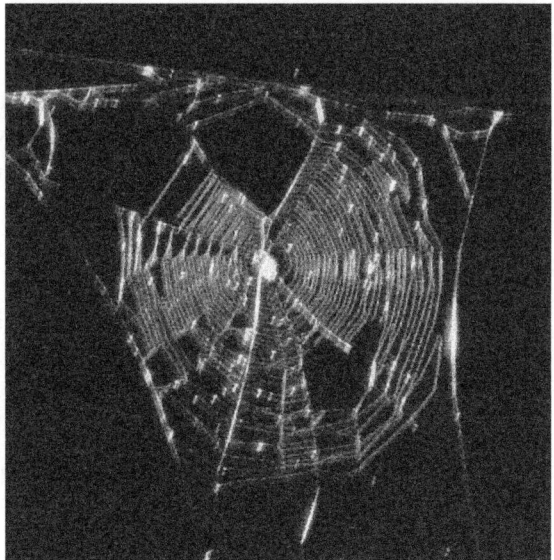

A spider web in front of a street light.

Standing Watch

It takes a special person to want to be a cop or a fireman; putting your life on the line every day for complete strangers. For these men and women, it's not just a job; it's who they are, and that desire to serve and protect is with them 24/7 as long as they're alive—and maybe even longer.

It was August of 1997, and Maureen Love of Tuxedo Park, N.Y. had just returned home from attending her uncle's funeral. Her uncle had served for 35 years in the New York City Fire Department, and he was also Maureen's godfather, so they had been especially close.

When she went to her car, it would not unlock and "the door lock switches started going up and down spasmodically"—which never happened before or after. Maureen finally had to call the front entry gate and ask for a police officer to get her car open.

The officer arrived a short time later "in a large, new SUV." Maureen and her husband commented on the big vehicle, which didn't seem appropriate for the often narrow, twisting and turning roads in Tuxedo Park.

"Oh that," the officer said with 'obvious disdain.' "We all hate it."

"So it was clear that no one in the department felt comfortable driving it," Maureen said. "But it wasn't until a few days later that I came to feel that this was all some sort of a warning from my recently deceased uncle that an accident was about to happen."

Just several days after the funeral, Maureen was on Route 17 headed north. As she approached the entry gate at Tuxedo Park, she saw lights flashing and realized that there must have been an accident. Once inside the gate, traffic was being rerouted, as there was an accident inside the park. As she drove along a road on the top of an embankment looking down onto Tuxedo Road, she saw police cars and a fire truck. Unfortunately, she also saw that the new police SUV was overturned, and a body was in the street.

As soon as she got home, Maureen called Father Cromey at St. Mary's Church (by the entry gate). She told him about the accident and urged him to get to the scene quickly to administer last rites, which he did.

The young police officer had been on routine patrol in the new SUV, when he began to pursue a speeder. Going around a curve, the vehicle flipped and rolled up the embankment. The officer was thrown from the vehicle—and then the large SUV rolled back down the embankment, pinning him underneath. The young officer, who had always dreamed of being a cop, died at the scene. The speeder was never caught.

A memorial service was held at St. Mary's, and a garden was created across the street with the officer's name carved into a memorial stone. And on the embankment where he died, a weeping beech tree was planted.

Over a decade after the accident, Maureen was driving home with a friend from a matinee performance of a play in Rockland County. It was once again August, and it was still light out.

"The play was really boring and my friend was napping in the car. When we got to the gate, we found that an enormous tree had come down across Tuxedo Road, and we were being diverted. There were a lot of police on the scene, and even the mayor was there."

Maureen drove along the detour, which took her to the site of the fatal accident so many years before. At this point, her friend was awake and commented, "Oh, the police are here, too."

"Where?" Maureen asked, not seeing anyone.

"Right over there," her friend replied, pointing.

"She was pointing to the corner diagonally across from where the young man died," Maureen explained. "I didn't see any police officers, so I asked her to describe him. She said he was very young, and basically described that officer! I felt it was like he was still there, protecting that street."

Maureen has thought a lot about all these incidents, along with other happenings that give her the sense that her uncle is still around. And she knows a thing or two about lingering spirits—her late husband, Tally, had been collecting accounts of Tuxedo ghost stories. He had held a few meetings at the Tuxedo Historical Society, where residents came to tell of their personal encounters. Unfortunately, no one recorded those sessions, but some people later wrote down their stories.

Once her friend saw that young officer, Maureen decided to write down all the details, and interview the police chief

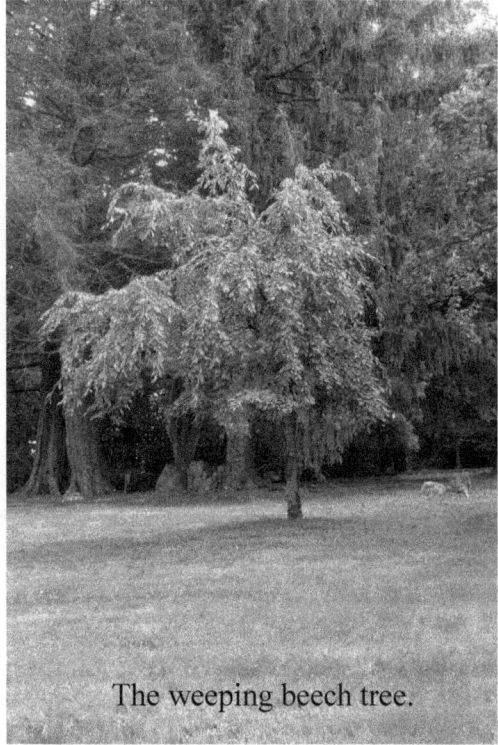

The weeping beech tree.

who was on duty the night of the accident. Even years later, she still believes the problems with her car were caused by her uncle trying to send a warning about the unstable SUV.

"He was trying to tell us that this vehicle is so dangerous, someone is going to get killed."

For all their apparent rivalry, cops and firemen have each other's backs when the going gets tough. Ultimately, they have the same job description—protect the public and offer aid to those in need. And these might just be jobs with no termination date.

Historic Haunts

In the spring of 2013, I was in Nanuet, NY to speak at a conference for high school students interested in local history. One of the other speakers was Rockland County Historian Craig Long, who I've had the pleasure of knowing for many years, and has always been very helpful with my projects on county history.

Craig handed me a large manila envelope, and said whenever he came across a local ghost story in an old newspaper, he made a copy of the article for me. I was delighted, as I love reading "new" cases from the past. As soon as I read the handful of clippings, I decided to include an entire chapter of these stories in the book.

At first, I thought it would amount to only a brief chapter at the end of the book, but then I started searching more newspapers, which led to a mini-obsession, and the chapter kind of grew in leaps and bounds. The stories are mostly local to the New York-New Jersey region, even though some of the articles may have appeared in newspapers from Nebraska or Kentucky! I was surprised how much national news ended up in small regional papers—yet didn't appear in any local papers!

I hope you enjoy these stories as much as I do. I have commented on many of them; some speak for themselves. It's fascinating to see how things have changed over the last century and a half, and how many things have stayed the same.

One glaring example is the way reporters make fun of people and their ghost stories, which unfortunately hasn't changed. One thing that fortunately has changed, for the most part, are the attitudes toward women, minorities, and foreigners, who are generally regarded as second-class citizens by reporters of the past.

Also, before delving into this chapter, realize that journalists rarely get all their facts straight these days. Whether or not newspapers of the past were more or less trustworthy is for you to decide. However, even the worst exaggerated accounts may hold kernels of paranormal truth.

The Rockland County Journal
January 19, 1870

The Bergen County Ghost

His Tuesday Evening Visits—Is Shot At, But Still Visits His Old Haunts—
The Neighborhood Excited—Suspicions Of A Mysterious Murder Having
Been Committed

To the Editor of the Journal:

We have at last something new in old Bergen. A new subject for discussion; something unaccountable, unnatural and marvelous. A real bona fide ghost has made its appearance at a hotel at Paramus, Bergen Co., N.J., and a crowd of people are visiting the premises weekly where his ghostship [this term is used like "his Lordship," not in regards to an actual ship] *appears. How long it has frequented the place is not known, but the present proprietor of the haunted hotel has lived there almost two years, and he asserts that it—the what is it?—has appeared regularly as long as he has lived there; and the supposition is that it was the ghostly visitant that drove the former occupants of the place away, as the hotel has frequently changed proprietors of late years.*

The fact of the place being haunted was kept quiet as long as possible, lest the report should injure the reputation of the house; but at last it has become known and it is now the theme of conversation and a subject of wonderment throughout the entire county.

Different persons who have stopped at the hotel over night have been placed in the haunted room for the evening, but having no knowledge of the fact that it was claimed by a ghost, and all of them have been frightened out of the room, and one of them was so beside himself as to jump from the window to the ground, a distance of fifteen feet.

There is one thing rather curious about it, and that is, it (the ghost) "revisits the glimpses of the moon" only on Tuesday night of each week and then it appears in the following manner: At about the hour of twelve— "that ghostly hour when churchyards yawn and graves give up their dead"—a wagon is heard to drive up to the door and stop. Someone alights, lets down the tail-board, walks into the house and up the stairs to a certain room, from which he soon issues and descending the stairs, drags, as it appears judging from the sound, a dead body after him. This he places in the wagon, makes everything secure and drives off.

Since the facts have become known to the public, numbers from all quarters have visited the premises; and a week ago a party of young men from New Bridge went up to see him, and did see him, and fired three shots at him, which, of course, had no other effect than to frighten themselves badly and send them all, pell mell, out of the room and off home sadder, if not wiser, men. Last Tuesday evening another crowd, numbering about seventy-five from all parts of Bergen county, gathered together to give his ghostship a reception, but whether they saw his highness or not, I cannot say. The probabilities are that they got outside of so much Jersey lightning that their visual organs became somewhat obscured and hence they were incapable of seeing everything.

There are rumors of a dark crime having been committed there at some time, and if a party of three or four gentlemen with nerves could have the house to themselves some evening and take measures to investigate the matter thoroughly, they might be able to throw some light on the subject. As things are at present, there certainly are grounds for the belief that there is something to be seen that is not of the "earth earthly," but what it is remains to be found out.

Your correspondent intends to screw his courage to the sticking point, and on some pleasant Tuesday evening visit the place and take possession of the room for the evening, with the determination to see the thing through, no matter in how "questionable shape" it may come; and then if he survives that night you may expect to hear more from

Anon.

Cresskill, January 10th, 1870.

The Weekly Kansas Chief
Thursday, May 1, 1873

Abe Lincoln's Ghost

A writer in Albany (N.Y.) Evening Times relates a conversation with a superstitious night watchman on the New York Central Railroad. Said the watchman: "I believe in spirits and ghosts. I know such things exist. If you will come in April I will convince you." He then told of the phantom train that every year comes up the road with the body of Abraham Lincoln. Regularly in the month of April about midnight, the air on the track becomes keen and cutting. On either side it is warm and still. Every watchman when he feels this air steps off the track and sits down to watch. Soon after the pilot engine, then long black streamers, and a band with black instruments, playing dirges, grinning skeletons sitting all about, will pass noiselessly, and the very air grows black. If it is moonlight clouds always come over the moon, and the music seems to linger as if frozen with horror. A few moments after and the phantom train glides by. Flags and streamers hang about. The track ahead seems covered with black carpet, and the wheels are draped with the same. The coffin of the murdered Lincoln is seen lying on the centre of the car, and all about in the air and train behind are vast numbers of blue-coated men, some with coffins on their backs, others leaning on them. It seems then that all the vast armies, that died during the war, are escorting the phantom train of the president. The wind if blowing dies away at once, and all the air is solemn hush, almost stifling, prevails. If a train were passing, its noise will be drowned in the silence, and the phantom train would ride over it. Clocks and watches always stop, and when looked at are found to be from five to eight minutes behind. Everywhere on the road about the 27th day of April, the time of watches and trains is found suddenly behind. This, said the leading watchman, was from the passage of the phantom train.

While this sounds like an elaborate work of fiction, I included it because the phantom Lincoln Funeral Train is one of the most widespread ghost stories in American history. The actual train left Washington, D.C. on April 21, 1865, and passed through 7 states and 180 cities over a distance of 1,654 miles before arriving in Springfield, Illinois where Lincoln was buried on May 4th. There were several scheduled stops where the coffin was taken to a public place to allow mourners to pay their respects, some waiting as long as five hours.

It wasn't long before people all across those 7 states started reporting the phantom funeral train on the anniversary of the date it passed those locations. Even well into the 20th century, the eyewitness accounts continued. While there were several variations, such as seeing a blinding white light as it passed, or a dense, black fog, the general descriptions of the train remained the same.

Unfortunately, the original train was destroyed in a fire in 1911, but there are plans to commemorate the 150th anniversary in 2015 with a replica of the funeral train following the same route from Washington, D.C. to Springfield, Illinois.

Will this new train have company along its route—perhaps from a train that stills the air, stops watches, and sends a deathly chill through all who see it?

Lincoln's Funeral Train in 1865

The Highland News
Albany, NY, July 15, 1875

A Ghost in Albany.

One evening, a week or two since, a lady residing in one of the southern wards was returning to her home, from a social gathering at a private house, near the hour of midnight. She was accompanied by a male relative who lived in the same house. As they were about to ascend the steps, both glanced upward toward the windows of the second story, and at one of them both saw, with perfect distinctness, a human face pressed against the pane. The features were not known to either, but presuming it to be a friend of their neighbor (as there was more than one family in the house), nothing strange was thought of it at the time. Before retiring, but after both had bared their feet, the lady and her companion bethought themselves of some article to be procured from the lower part of the house, and as its location was known, they descended without a light. On returning, just as the young gentleman placed his foot upon the landing at the head of the stairs, he felt beneath it a yielding substance, the shape of which was so clearly defined that he exclaimed: "Why, aunty, I stepped on somebody's thumb!" At the same instant the lady, putting down her foot, responded: "I have stepped on the hand." No sounds of retreating footsteps were heard, and such examination as the darkness permitted failed to discover any human being near them. On procuring a light, a moment later, both soon satisfied themselves that no creature of flesh and blood was in the immediate vicinity. Wondering and trembling at the contact of these mysteries, the witnesses retired to their beds.

In the morning, a simple inquiry, which attracted no attention, elicited the fact that there had been no living person in the house other than the usual members of the family, and a critical comparison of the features of each one with the face she had seen, a sharp impression of which was fixed in her mind, convinced the lady that it was not that of any one of them.

The most startling and mysterious of the phenomena remains to be told. As if to convince them that their imaginations had not been worked upon by any means to create the impression we have detailed, there appeared upon the bottom of the gentleman's foot the next morning, plainly printed, in a color quite like blood red, the fac-simile of the thumb he had felt beneath it, and upon the foot of the lady was as clearly discernible the likeness of the inside of a human hand.—*Albany (N. Y.) Argus.*

This is one of those strange little stories that is low on facts and is just ripe to become one of those urban legends—*The Tale of the Bloody Thumb*, or something like that. Still, two people saw a face in the window and later stepped on something that left its mark. And somehow it made it into the newspaper!

Rockland County Journal
Down in New Jersey
March 10, 1877

They have a ghost that is frightening people near Park Ridge.

Rockland County Journal
Saturday, November 29, 1879

A brakeman on the Erie was frightened nearly into spasms the other night by what he said was a ghost, near Sterling Junction, the spot where a brakeman named Fitz was killed recently.

Rockland County Journal
Suffern, January 19, 1881

The ghost has been seen again—this time by a party returning from a fishing excursion. According to all accounts his ghostship is making too frequent visits to this place of late.

City and Country
August 24, 1883

Ramapo

Four carloads of excursionists from Paterson picnicked on the old quarantine ground at Hillburn on Tuesday.

The Viola Sabbath School visited the grove on Wednesday and enjoyed a very pleasant day.

Lovers of the "national game" would like to see another exhibition of skill such as that evinced by our home club and the Spring Valley Lawn Tennis Club in their recent match game played here.

A ghost has made its appearance here; a rather lively one, too, for it chased a young man a considerable distance on Sunday night, and vanished into the air on attempting to cross the bridge. It looked like a woman dressed in white, but might have been a shadow.

August 31, 1883

Mr. Charles Malloy and Miss Laura Clark were married on Saturday evening. Their many friends extend congratulations.

The ghost has not appeared again. All are curious to know its identity.

Our village has been unusually quiet this season—cause, no summer boarders.

I love the way they just lump all the news together. I also found it interesting that they referred to tennis as the national game, not baseball. Of course, what was most interesting was the apparition in white that chased someone and then vanished at the bridge. I also shook my head over the offered excuse of a shadow, even though the figure was described as being a woman in a white dress—which is a lot of detail if it was just a shadow!

Rockland County Journal
Suffern, NY, February 9, 1884

Two of the extra brakemen of the Erie, on a recent visit to our town, had an interview with the ghost. One of them was so frightened that he became paralyzed for a time and fell to the ground. The other one left his partner and ran. After a time things became quiet again, and the two visitors left town on the milk train.

Rockland County Journal
Hillburn, February 16, 1884

James Butler, the milk dealer, of Suffern, came in contact with the ghost one
evening last week.

Rockland County Journal
March 19, 1887

The ghost of Moses, the peddler, who
was reported to have been run over and
killed at Tappan, has been seen in this
place within the past few weeks. Some
persons are foolish enough to believe that
the man himself is still alive, and the *City
and Country* last week suffered from a
half column of painful lamentations over
the wickedness of correspondents. We
wonder whether Moses supplied our re-
spected contemporary with neckties and
suspenders, "tree for a quarter." Alas !
poor Moses.

Considerable excitement has prevailed among some of the residents of Piermont lately over an alleged ghost which, it is claimed, perambulates the road from D. W. Kipp's store to Haddock's Hall and back, and frightens the people who are so unfortunate, or so fortunate, as to see his ghostship. Of course, the most of the people in our sister village doubted the story of the ghost when they were first told it, and claimed that the frightened persons had been imbibing too much; but an investigation proves that nothing but birch beer and weakened soda water are sold at Piermont, and our friends of Sparkill, when they desire to go on a "lark," can find nothing in their village to drink but creek water and pennyroyal tea, so the ghost certainly did not have his birth in a bottle. The "imbibing" theory thus being upset, the ghost must be accepted as a real spectre, bent on a mission at present to us unknown.

The most authentic story we have yet heard concerning the alleged ghost was told us by Counsellor William E. Gowdey, who thinks he knows a ghost when he sees one, and we believe he does. "I have had considerable experience in this line," said the counsellor, "and the happiest moments of my life are when I can go at midnight into a cemetery and walk around in the place where ghosts are supposed to be raised. This Sparkill ghost is a gen-

uine spook ; I know whereof I speak, for
I have seen it. You needn't look at me so
suspiciously," continued friend Gowdey,
"for I'm a temperance man and have not
taken anything. You may mention my
name as authority for what I say. I was
within three or four feet of the ghost the
other night, and have seen it several
times. It is very tall, and is sometimes
dressed in white, sometimes in black.
You can state authoritatively that I have
seen the Pierpont ghost and know it is
genuine."

Justice Slocum was very reticent in regard to the matter. He did not give his
opinion, but wore a look of great seriousness. The fact that he was seen early on
Monday afternoon walking
the haunted road on his way to Sparkill
is pretty good evidence that he was hunting for traces of the spook. We shall see
him later in regard to the matter.

We believe a further investigation is
going to be made into the ghost mystery.

Omaha Daily Bee
Sunday, April 29, 1888

Driven Out by a Ghost

Albany, N.Y. Journal: The latest sensation at Little Falls, N.Y., is a haunted house, and many believers in "spooks" actually think that the terrified people that were frightened have the best of reasons to vacate the dwelling, which they did without much delay. No. 29 Porteus street is a dwelling occupied by two families, that of James Carney on the first floor, and Mrs. Moynahan, a widow, and her children on the second. These families have occupied the house for the past two months.

Of late they have been startled by ghostly and unusual noises, such as a dry, sepulchral cough and the slamming and opening of doors. If a door was closed it would suddenly spring open without the aid of visible hands, and if it was open it would close with a slam in the same mysterious ways. In one of the rooms occupied by the Carneys after dark the dry coughing commences, so ghostlike in sound, as Mr. Carney describes it, it makes the hair rise on the head, and can be distinctly heard all night long, and apparently comes from under the bed.

Doors locked at night are found unlocked in the morning, and yet there are no signs that a human hand had unfastened them. The families being unable to solve the mystery of these ghostly manifestations have vacated the house. Last Monday night the coughing and opening and closing of the doors so demoralized them that they took refuge in one room. There were seven in all, but still the ghost was not disturbed by their presence, for it kept coughing and making peculiar noises the entire night, and the coughing always proceeded from the same spot under the bed.

It was a long and fearful night, and the inmates of the haunted house clung to each other and waited with beating hearts and terror in their souls for the break of day, when the invisible spirit would vanish. With its disappearance the coughing ceased. The night was one long to be remembered, and they shiver now when they think of it. The following day after their unusual experience the premises were vacated.

Omaha Daily Bee
Sunday, April 29, 1888

Policemen Terrified by Hobgoblins

Pensacola (Fla) correspondence St. Louis Globe Democrat: A short time since two foreign sailors were drowned in the harbor here, and the stevedores say that their ghosts walk, and nothing can induce the majority of them to go near the wharves at midnight. A dozen sailors of a British vessel lying at anchor a quarter of a mile from shore came ashore on liberty, and, like all Jack-tars, had a jolly time, ending by getting drunk as so many lords. Two of them missed the return boat, and on going down at midnight, found out that they were left. Being just far enough "over seas" not to know the dangers of the strong tides, they undressed and plunged in to swim out to the ship, leaving their clothes on the wharf. Some negroes passing by stole the clothes. The next day the bodies of the two men were cast ashore a mile below town.

The second day after a negro came into the police station, and handing the captain a package, told him that it contained the clothing of the two sailors. The negro added that the men who had taken them had given them to him to return, as the ghosts of the two men had appeared to them in nature's garb, and with horrible imprecations demanded their clothes. The frightened thieves did not dare to keep them after this, and returned them at once.

The chief laughed at the tale, and putting the clothes to one side, thought little more of it. The next day the patrol who was stationed at the central wharf, where the sailors left from asked for a change of station, alleging that the cold night air from off the water was bad for him. He was given another post and a different officer given the beat. He, too, applied for a change, and successively six different officers gave up the place. The chief then investigated and told the following story:

"At about 11:30 the attentions of the policeman on duty was attracted by a noise like as if a swimmer was climbing up the side of the wharf. Suspecting thieves had hastened there, and opening his bulls-eye lantern he threw his light on the spot where the noise was heard. As the rays illuminated the dock there stepped into the circle of light the ghostly forms of the dead sailors magnified to huge proportions, stark naked, seaweed clinging to their hair, and their faces and bodies horribly eaten by fish and crabs. They stalked the officer without seeming to notice him, and going to the spot where their clothes had been left, appeared to be hunting for something—their vain search seeming to render them perfectly furious with rage. The officer dropped his lantern and fled. The others all corroborated his tale and related the same general experience, save the last one, who added to his story that one of the spectral figures came up and had attempted to embrace him, with a drunken leer on its-corpse-like face. No officer stationed there now and not a negro in the city would go on the dock at midnight for $1,000. During the day hundreds of people have visited the spot and commented upon the strange tale. The officers *are laughed at by many, but they stick to their story and refuse to do duty on that particular wharf.*

Was this a case of mass hysteria? Were the two men who stole the clothes influenced by guilt and fear when they discovered the clothes were from drowned sailors? Had this story spread through the police force, wreaking havoc on their imaginations?

It's hard to believe that eight police officers would risk ridicule, and their jobs, by fabricating and sticking to such stories. If there is a shred of truth to their accounts, then is it possible that these sailors were so drunk they didn't even realize they were dead, and kept returning to find their clothes?

Nyack Journal
Tuesday, August 6, 1889

A GHOST!

A WEIRD SPECTRE ACTUALLY SEEN IN NYACK

We learn from undoubted authority that our friend A.W. Tallman, actually saw a ghost some distance north of the Nyack station at a late hour the other night, and at once reported the fact to Night Watchman Degroat. The last-named gentleman secured a shot-gun, went up in the yard, and blazed away at the spectre. It is said that the air was filled with sulphurous smoke, Messers. Tallman's and Degroat's hair stood on end for a moment. Then the leaves on the trees became motionless, the breeze died away, the sulphur vanished, and all was as silent as the graveyard.

The ghost has not since been seen.

That's quite an account! I wish there had been some description of what the ghost had looked like, and why the watchman felt the need to shoot at it! I assume the "sulphurous smoke" was something not related to the shotgun, as the smell made their hair stand on end. And the fact that these two men were willing to go on record with their story speaks to the fact that something frightened both of them enough to speak out publicly.

There was another article that appeared two days later, but this account didn't seem to be as credible to the writer, since he didn't personally know the "young man" as he did Mr. Tallman, but still found it worth reporting.

Nyack Journal
Thursday, August 8, 1889

ANOTHER GHOST!

BUT THE STORY IS NOT WELL AUTHENTICATED

Since Mr. A.W. Tallman's experience with a ghost the other night, we have been told another ghost story which does not appear to be well authenticated. Of course, the JOURNAL does not wish to exaggerate in regard to ghosts and would not fabricate on the subject under any circumstances. However, we give the story as we received it:

A young man returning home shortly after eleven o'clock pm on Monday night, says when he turned the corner of DeCantillon Avenue and Franklin Street he saw a large object in white, a little north of the corner, waving its hands and making a motion as if coming towards him. His hair stood on end for a moment, and giving a leap he started on a brisk run down Franklin Street. At the corner of North Street he met a friend, and with him returned to the place where the ghostly object was seen, but it had disappeared.

Now this is the story as we have it, and the young man says it is true.

With so few details it's hard to determine if there's any truth to this story, or had someone just been spooked after reading the article about the ghost just two days earlier? Also, I had never heard of DeCantillon Avenue, and found that it had later been renamed Haven Court. I haven't found any reference as to where North Street was located.

Nyack Evening Journal
Wednesday, May 24, 1893

PETER AND THE GHOST

HE THINKS HIS NEIGHBORHOOD HAUNTED BY SPIRITS

But When He Offers to Shoot the Ghost Full of Holes, the Noise Ceases

Peter Goepfert, the well-known news dealer on Franklin street, is not at all superstitious, but recent occurrences set him thinking for a time about spirits which are said to appear in the solemn hour of midnight. Everybody knows that Peter is a good, honest citizen, and why spooks should revel in his neighborhood in the solemn stillness of night nobody knows.

One night after Peter and his wife had retired, they heard a noise which sounded for all the world like spirits rapping at a séance. They could not account for the strange demonstration, but finally succeeded in getting asleep. The next night the noise was repeated, and for several nights afterward the weird sounds repeated.

"I am not afraid of ghosts," said Peter to a friend. "I fought in too many battles before I came to this country to be afraid of such things; but the noise puzzled me for a time. Then I resolved to investigate."

Peter did make an investigation and it was a remarkably successful one. "If I find them ghosts," said he, "I will show them that they musn't fool around Peter." So when at midnight that night the usual spirit rappings were heard, Peter rushed out to the spot whence the noise proceeded, and there, he says, he found a large, real, live ghost dressed in white.

"I will shoot you full of holes if you keep on with this noise," said Peter, having his revolver with him; and then the ghost disappeared. "I haven't heard anything more of the ghost," said he to a friend, "and I guess it must have been scared away. No, no, I ain't afraid of no ghost," continued he, "and it won't be healthy for the spook to appear again. I tell you, when people play tricks on me, they will get the worst of it. If that

106

ghost comes around here again, it will go away full of holes, for I will shoot."

Well, clearly I've been wasting time with EMF meters and infrared cameras—all I need to do is bring guns to my next investigation and threaten to shoot any ghost that moves!

This may very well have been someone playing a prank on Peter, but while it may have been fun the first night or two, would someone really go out in the dead of night over and over again to tap on something? And it's interesting to note how commonplace "spirit rappings at a séance" must have been in that age of spiritualism, as the reporter assumes everyone knows what he means.

And finally, I laughed out loud when I read Peter's statement, "I ain't afraid of no ghost." A 19th century Ghostbuster!

Nyack Evening Journal
Saturday, August 12, 1893

TWO FEMININE "SPOOKS"

A COUPLE OF NYACK BOYS BADLY FRIGHTENED

While Passing the New Cemetery Entrance,
They Are Greeted by Startling Apparitions

While people may generally discredit ghost stories, there are two young men in Nyack who are to-day firm believers in the materialization of departed spirits, and if they fail to get to their full growth in the next two or three years it will be because of a serious fright received by them last night.

The young men referred to, who made an urgent appeal to have their names kept out of this paper, went to a house on the old Rockland Lake road, not far from the Bedell corner, early last evening to spend a few hours with the female portion of the family. They left the place on their return shortly after 11 o'clock, coming down Highland avenue, and intending to strike into Midland avenue on the north side of Tillou's woods. They changed their plans somewhat, however, and continued down past the new cemetery entrance, west of the ball field. As the young men reached the point where the new cemetery gate is to be, one of them began joking about ghosts. Both laughed heartily, when suddenly two large figures clothed in ghostly raiment rose up before them from the side of the road. Here was a severe test of courage, and the young men were not equal to the emergency. They gave a single bound across the road, struck into the path which leads through the old ball field, and ran as they never ran before, not stopping once until they halted under the electric light at the corner of Main street and Midland avenue.

The scared young men insist upon it that they saw a couple of genuine ghosts, but other persons who were in the neighborhood at the time say that a couple of girls dressed in white were sitting by the roadside with their lovers, and when they heard the young men speaking of ghosts, they thought they would give them a scare, succeeding beyond their expectations.

Hard to believe these two young men were so terrified by a couple of girls essentially saying "Boo," but the streets of Nyack were probably rather dark in 1893—except for "the electric light at the corner of Main street and Midland avenue"—so anything is possible.

Normally, I would dismiss this as a prank, but the "new cemetery entrance" they were passing must have been at Oak Hill Cemetery, one of the most haunted places in Rockland County. (See my book *Ghosts of Rockland County*.) Seeing apparitions in the dead of night in this cemetery is nothing unusual.

Still, with so little information, we can't determine if there just happened to be two girls dressed in white late at night at just the right spot to jump out and scare these boys, or was this just a handy excuse to explain the sighting?

The Evening Times
Thursday, July 15, 1897

SCARED BY A GHOST"S EMBRACE

A Kingston Lady Avers She Was Hugged By A Spirit

Kingston, N.Y., July 15. –Old "Squire" Josiah Dubois has long been dead, and his house has remained unoccupied. Weeds grew in the yard and vines covered the windows, while the birds made nests in the eaves. The house was haunted and people were afraid to live in it.

Mr. Dubois, who was a spiritualist, often said that when he died he would return to his home. In the dead of night strange sounds could be heard in the deserted house, and the neighbors gave it a wide berth.

This month Mr. and Mrs. Daniel Burke came to live there with their child and the noises ceased.

Last night Mrs. Burke took her child and went down to Kingston Point, a summer resort near by, and returned quite late in the evening. Entering her home she went into the parlor to lock the windows. Suddenly her husband, who was asleep in the next room, heard a frightful shriek, and, rushing out, found his wife senseless on the floor, her child crouching over her. It was a long time before Mrs. Burke was restored to consciousness.

She said that she started to go into the bedroom, when a man in a white robe, with a long white beard and dark eyes, grabbed and hugged her.

Mrs. Burke, who never saw Squire Dubois, described him exactly as her apparition.

Great story! I wonder if the Burkes moved elsewhere after this frightening encounter, and whether the Dubois house still stands today? I did find a record of a Josiah Dubois born in 1823, who died in 1895, which would tie into the 1897 haunting timeline. He is buried in Montrepose Cemetery in Kingston—although his spirit may still be wandering.

NOTE: Many thanks to Osheana Chaneyfield for searching the huge cemetery for Josiah Dubois' grave. She did find many Dubois gravestones, but none with the discernible name of Josiah. (Some were unreadable.)

Thanks also to Bobbi Nelson for her research into the Dubois family.

Rockland County Journal
January 14, 1889

GHOST MAKES TROUBLE

Herman Paul Schultz, the first man to be hanged in Pike Co., made lots of trouble for the authorities while living and continues to make trouble for them now that he is dead. According to a dispatch from Stroudsburg to the N. Y. *Sun*, the disembodied spirit of Mr. Schultz on Christmas night made a social call on Jeffrey Van Tassell, a stonecutter from Parker's Glen, who was sleeping off the effects of a jay in the cell formerly occupied by Schultz in the Milford jail. The ghost was inclined to be sociable, but the stonecutter emitted a series of yells that aroused everybody within a radius of half a mile and then the supernatural visitor disappeared.

This is fascinating, as Mike and I have been to this building in Milford, PA, where Schultz was held for the murder of his wife—as well as hung, *inside the courthouse*! The article fails to mention that this was not just Schultz's place of imprisonment, but the site of his death, as well, which makes the possibility of a haunting more likely. Also, when the noose was placed around his neck, he complained that the rope tickled and asked for it to be loosened, which was a grave mistake. The loose rope failed to snap his neck and bring an instant death. Instead, he slowly suffocated while twisting in midair.

In another strange twist, so to speak, in 2009, Mike and I had one of our most remarkable investigations at The Columns Museum in Milford. (See *Ghost Investigator Volume 9*). As soon as we entered the building, Mike complained of having some bad pains in his neck. Shortly after, he found a display case that held a noose and shackles—the noose and shackles used in Schultz's execution! It appears as though this murderer left some lasting impressions even after death.

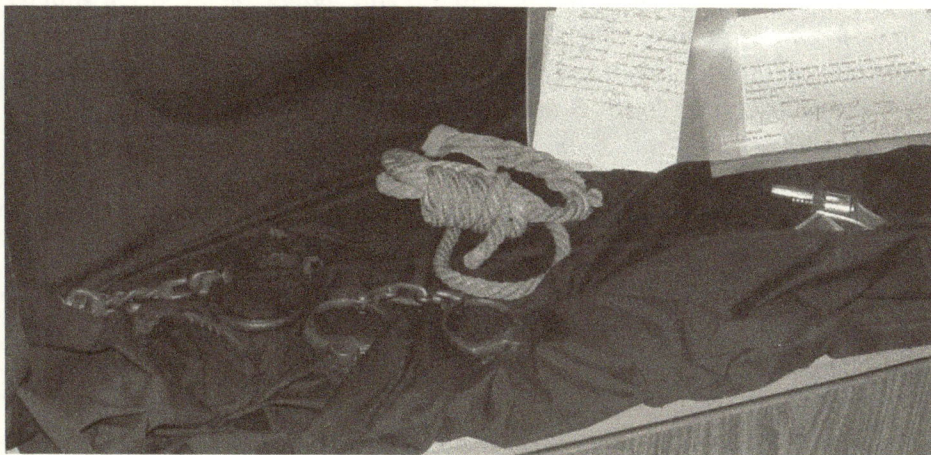

The shackles and noose used to hang Schultz. The gun on the right was the one Schultz used to shoot his wife. In addition to this gruesome display, The Columns has the flag used to cushion Lincoln's head when he was shot in Ford's Theater, and the flag still has Lincoln's blood stains. This building also has a female ghost who was the strongest I ever encountered.

Nyack Evening Star
Tuesday, March 26, 1901

A PIERMONT YARN

Story About a Girl's Spirit Haunting House She Died in

What do you think? They've got a ghost, a real ghost, down at Piermont. Lots of people down that way have been much worked up about it for two days past. The Bradbury brothers and their families, in particular, have, been much wrought up about it. The ghost dwells in a stone wall at the rear of the Bradbury families' home. They live in the Masonic building. Members of the family take the thing real seriously. This spectre that has spread acute insomnia among them, is a white robed figure of a girl, who at different and varying hours of the night quietly glides from out of the stone wall referred to and walks through the back door into the house. When this ghostly apparition gets in the house the big Bradburys and the little Bradburys scamper to cover. That is, it is presumed they do, because one of the Bradbury "boys" could not tell what becomes of the white robed spirit after it gets in doors.

There were hundreds of people (hundreds is reported to be correct) at the old Masonic building Saturday and Sunday nights, looking for the ghost. Superstitious people (they exist in this era) believe the ghost to be the spirit of a young woman who died in the "haunted" building several years ago.

What a fascinating story, and I can just imagine the crowds of people waiting in breathless anticipation for the ghost to appear!

I particularly like this next story for two reasons: It's a great story, and this reporter actually thinks the debunker's excuse was absurd.

The Minneapolis Journal
Yonkers, NY, April 2, 1901

Best Ghost Story of the Year

Yonkers, N. Y., has one of the best authenticated ghost stories of the year. Miss Julia Murray, a talented woman of that city, died a few days ago of meningitis. The next morning at 4 a. m., while a number of her friends and relatives were sitting up with the body, as is the custom in many places, there appeared near the wall in one corner of the next room the form of the dead girl. Miss Katie Kane, a cousin of Miss Murray, screamed and dropped to her knees. In the room at the time was Miss Nora Smith, who fainted when she saw the apparition, and Miss Rose and Miss Jennie McGowan, daughters of James McGowan. When Miss Kane screamed it attracted Miss Rose Kearns, Mrs. James Corbads and William Murray from the next room. They, with the Misses McGowan and Miss Kane, watched the vision. It remained near the wall about five minutes and then slowly disappeared. The body of the dead girl lay in the next room.

The story was carefully investigated by three of the New York papers and no flaw could be found in it. One of these papers finally sent Garitt P. Serviss, the well-known scientist, to investigate further. Mr. Serviss had a nice little theory all worked out on paper that the vision was a reflection from the mirror. To his disgust he found that all the mirrors in the house were shrouded in cloth, a custom in some families when a death occurs in the house. Besides this, the body of the dead girl was in another room.

Mr. Serviss then fell back on the theory of "contagious hallucination." That is, one of the watchers had a hallucination of the dead girl's ghost and six others "caught it," one so violently that she fainted. This theory is so obviously worked up to get rid of the facts that it has little standing in common sense. In spite of the desperate attempts made to explain away all these numerous facts of the so-called borderland between life and death, it is impossible to get away from the conviction that there is a mass of crude fact that has not yet been sufficiently digested or organized to make it into a science but which contains valuable material.

City and Country
Saturday, July 28, 1906

THE "SPOOK HOUSE" SOLD

Middletown, July 25.—The "spook house" on Benton avenue, this city, occupied by Luther R. Marsh, the noted lawyer, in his declining years, was sold today, to Dr. B.B. Kinne, of Philadelphia, who will turn the mansion into a sanitarium. Some weeks ago an effort was made to sell the property at public sale, but no bidders appeared, although the property is a most desirable one. Superstitious people said the house was haunted.

The property belonged to the estate of Clarissa J. Huyler, the medium who, it is charged, for years duped the venerable Luther R. Marsh. It was here that Mrs. Huyler dictated the greater part of one of Mr. Marsh's well known books, "The Voice From the Patriarchs." Mrs. Huyler called to earth the spirits of many Bible characters and Marsh communed with them, putting their words in his book.

This is not just a ghost story, it is a cautionary tale. Luther R. Marsh was a prominent lawyer. To give an example of his caliber, the famous Daniel Webster joined his firm. He was living comfortably with his fortune in Massachusetts, when Clarissa Huyler read about Marsh's interest in spiritualism. It was then she hatched a plot to bring Marsh to Middletown, New York, and slowly drain him of his wealth while pretending that spirits were guiding her.

Mr. Huyler, after the death of his wife, told the whole story of her scam, and how she duped the brilliant old lawyer out of houses, property, cash, and diamonds. Marsh lived with Mrs. Huyler in a house he bought for her on Benton Avenue, a house that had a "Spirit Room" were séances regularly took place. The fraudulent medium made sure Marsh stayed in the house and isolated him from his friends. She was certain that the elderly Marsh would die first and she would enjoy the spoils of her deceit.

However, as fate would have it, Mrs. Huyler died first, and Marsh was free to enjoy the company of his friends once again, until he died in the house in 1902 and the age of eighty-nine.

Perhaps Marsh's spirit then haunted the place, trapped by remorse for being so gullible? Could the ghost have been that of Mrs. Huyler, now on the other side of the séance, trying to vindicate herself about the existence of the spirit world? Or, was this house's haunted reputation just the result of all the alleged spirit contacts over the years?

I would love to visit the place and find out for myself, but as there is currently no mansion at the address on Benton Avenue, I assume it was demolished for the row of more modest houses that stand on the site today. I wonder if any of the residents there know of the strange history of this place, and if any of them have "inherited" the ghosts?

Appearing in both the
New York Tribune
August 3, 1907
and
Daily Press
Newport News, VA, August 4, 1907

DOG'S GHOST BUSY IN SUFFERN

Doctor's Dead Pet Said to Annoy Residents Near His Grave

SUFFERN, N.Y., Aug. 3—The alleged ghost of a dead dog is annoying residents here in River street. They say the animal interferes with their slumbers at night and frightens them in the daytime. The dog was the property of Dr. Gilbert Johnston, and it died three weeks ago.

The physician was attached to the animal, and attended to the burial. Since that time complaints of noise have been made daily, and the River street residents say the barking and yelping comes from the dog's grave. Only one man backs up the complainants. He says he visited the spot and heard the noises attributed to the animal. Dr. Johnston's neighbors insist that the dog's body be disinterred.

What can you say about this sad story? There have certainly been many reports of animal ghosts, but this one is particularly disturbing—the poor dog was heard by many people barking at its own gravesite! And you have to love that the neighbors were insisting that the doctor dig up the dead dog!

Kingston Daily Freeman
July 24, 1907

Glasco has a Ghost

THE SPOOK IS THAT OF A MUR-DERED ITALIAN.

The ghost has been walking in Glasco, and according to some of the stories that have been told it was the ghost of John Sacco, who was murdered there last winter. The ghost was seen several weeks ago hovering around the spot where he became a ghost, and a number of the Italian residents were badly frightened. Recently the ghost has failed to appear, and it is hoped that he has returned to his former home in Italy, or else has been so affected by the weather that he will remain where all good ghosts should.

As usual, this reporter is making fun of the story. It would have been nice to show a little respect for a man who had been brutally murdered just several months earlier. According to newspaper articles from December

1906-January 1907, the murder was the result of a dispute that arose with a neighbor, Antonio Cahvelli, over all things, a bag of manure!

Cahvelli shot Sacco in the head four times in rapid succession, paused, then shot him a fifth time. The five .38 caliber bullets created "a big hole, from which blood and brains oozed." Cahvelli then had the nerve to go to Sacco's house and chat with his wife for several hours, pretending to be waiting for Sacco so they could get some beer.

If anyone had the right to become a restless spirit, it was John Sacco!

Nyack Journal
Thursday, August 27, 1908

HERE'S A GHOST STORY.

Spook Reported in a Home at Grand View.

TALE TOLD IN A CITY PAPER

*The Blauvelt Home Given Fame as
the Alleged Abiding Place of Mysterious Wraith*

The following ghost story appeared in this morning's New York Herald, and readers may take it for what it is worth:

"In one of the beautiful old houses overlooking the Hudson, at Grand View, near South Nyack, there's a ghost—not the common variety of wraith that inhabits dusty attics, but a most active apparition that sits bolt upright on a sofa in broad daylight, walks unbidden into the bathroom, tumbles the soap and towels about, turns on the water, turns off the lights, causes doors to open and shut, and does sundry and diverse things that nothing but a real ghost could do, and a capable ghost at that.

"This uncanny visitor makes his appearance in the residence of Mr. and Mrs. J.M. Blauvelt, who occupy one of those fine old houses on the west bank of the Hudson. It has a beautiful lawn, grand old shade trees and large airy rooms, which overlook the water. The Blauvelts are reckoned among the good people of the Hudson Valley, and not the sort to be seeing unnatural things; nevertheless Mrs. Blauvelt and their butler, Cornelius Radcliff, have been so persistently confronted by the ghost within the last month or two that there is little sleep or pleasure left for them anywhere."

Wow, that's my idea of a haunting! As the article doesn't give the address of the house, I looked at the 1910 census and did find J. M. Blauvelt, who would have been 53 in 1908. I wonder if this house is still standing, and if this restless spirit is still active?

The following is not a ghost story, but it is so bizarre I couldn't resist including it. Could you imagine living in a crypt!?

Hartford Herald
Wednesday, March 22, 1911

TWO TRAMP PRINTERS NOT AFRAID OF GHOSTS

Nyack, N. Y., March 18.— Two men describing themselves as tramp printers, are under arrest here, charged by the police with having made their home for the greater part of the winter in a vault in the Rockland cemetery.

The men are said to have lived for nearly three months in the dark, damp room, measuring 10 by 12 feet.

Their improvised bed of straw and blankets was spread upon two coffins, and funeral urns afforded a storehouse for their food.

The McCook tribune
June 8, 1900

Ghost Played Piano.

West Point correspondent New York Herald: Residents of Rugertown, a suburb of the post, are interested in a weird concert which was given one night this week in the parlor of the home of Andrew Kuhn, a private of the army service detachment. The performance did not begin until just as the old clock in the tower of the academic building had struck the hour of midnight, the artist was invisible, and ghostly sonatas, symphonies and the like were rendered in wonderful style. It seems that Kuhn, who is an old resident of the post, had retired with his family for the night, when they were aroused by very loud and thrilling piano playing. The sound seemed to be coming from the parlor. Upon their entering the room they found it quite deserted. The piano lid was closed, but some invisible agency was sounding the keys. They were badly frightened. It might have been a cat, but the piano was closed, or it might have been rats nibbling the strings, but the strings have been found to be uninjured.

One question: Since when do cats or rats play sonatas and symphonies?

The Evening World
August 1, 1919

Spry Ghost Foils Cops in Yonkers

Six Families Report Night Visitor Floats in Air and Grabs Bedclothes

The Police Department of the city of Yonkers is engaged in an effort to lay hold a ghost—a ghost which yanks bedclothes off beds and jumps from the roof to the yard of a three-story apartment and, presumably, jumps back again, because it has been seen going in both directions, and emits long drawn-out, hollow echoing moans, which cause the blood of listeners to run cold.

Occupants of the apartment house owned by Joseph Schwartz at No. 436 Walnut Street, in the Nodine Hill district, are convinced that such a ghost is camping in their midst and announce that if the police are unable to evict it they will have to move.

Schwartz visited Police Headquarters in Yonkers yesterday and hesitatingly approached Lieut. Dennis Cooper. The landlord is a sensible man, and he opened up by requesting the lieutenant not to laugh at him.

"I came here," said Schwartz, "to complain about a ghost. For some time past the six families in my apartment house have been complaining that a ghost is making their lives miserable. I didn't pay much attention at first, but the complaints multiplied and I went up there and heard and saw things which lead me to believe there is something in what my tenants are worrying about. As a taxpayer and a citizen I ask for a police investigation."

Lieut. Cooper sent Detective Sergt. Lewis Ford and Detective Patrick Flood out to the house. The two sleuths interviewed all the tenants who were home and found the people were quite serious and considerably disturbed.

Mrs. Josephine Bushell is one of the tenants who has seen whatever it is that has been disturbing the people in the house. When she first began to hear the noises in the halls and in the cellar and on the roof and apparently in the walls she tried to locate the cause, but she hasn't done

121

any exploring lately. She quit when one night a few days ago, she saw something white flash by her window as though bound from the roof to the ground. She heard no sound and ran to the window and looked out, but saw nothing beneath.

Mrs. Bushell told detectives a woman burned to death in the house many years ago. She thinks the ghost of this unfortunate woman has come back.

Mrs. Fannie Sperger never saw the ghost, but has heard it moan and move around many times. She told the detective about John Zeust, who lived in the house up to a few days ago. His furniture is still there, but he sleeps elsewhere.

Zeust, she said, was alone in his apartment last Sunday night. His wife was visiting in the country. It was just at midnight and Zeust was asleep. The window was open. Suddenly, the bedclothes were yanked off the bed and he awoke to see something white flitting through the window and floating upward until it was lost to view.

Ford and Flood reported to headquarters and Detectives Ciliberti and John McCormack were instructed to go to the house last night and prospect for the ghost. They hid in the lower hall until shortly after midnight when they heard moans and sounds they were unable to identify apparently in the public hall on the second floor. Noiselessly they hurried up, but found nothing on that floor or anywhere else in the house. They remained around until daylight and returned to headquarters to report.

Lieut. Dennis Cooper is determined to get that ghost if he has to go after it himself.

Another story about this case appeared the next day:

New York Tribune
August 2, 1919

Yonkers Police Sent to Get Ghost, Dead or Alive

Yonkers, Aug. 1—The police here have been ordered to get the ghost, dead or alive, that is disturbing residents at 436 walnut Street.

It's a noisy ghost, filling the neighborhood with groans and moans, and eerie shrieks all night long, and it has a mean disposition, too, for, according to residents, it sneaks up on persons innocently sleeping and steals their bedclothes.

Detectives Pasquale Ciliberti and John McCormack were assigned to catch the ghost last night. They entered the building with many expressions of skepticism and left an hour or so later with their hair resembling the fretful porcupine. For the rest of the night they patrolled outside of the building, but they didn't see the ghost come out. Additional police will mount guard to-night.

The Sun also had an article on August 2nd, detailing the same story, except they quote Mrs. Bushell as saying that a mother and her daughter had been burned to death in the house. Unfortunately, I was unable to find any additional articles, so I don't know if the tenants moved out, if the ghost found peace, or if the cops kept running away looking like frightened porcupines!

An element of this story reminds me of a place I visited and wrote about in *America's Historic Haunts*, the Heathman Hotel in Portland, Oregon. It's a beautiful hotel, with a dark secret—someone jumped from the roof to their death, and all the rooms he passed on the way down now experience paranormal activity!

Did the woman or child who died in this apartment building in the fire, actually jump from the roof? That might account for the white shape plunging down and being seen by the windows. In any event, this is a fascinating story involving multiple eyewitnesses, at least two previous deaths that could be the cause of the haunting, and significant police involvement.

Journal News
Saturday, January 29, 1938

GHOST WALKS AIRILY ABOUT NANUET HOME

*Disembodied Spirit of Girl Who Once
Aspired to Be Dancer Floats*

As the Mist, People Say

"Tap-tap-tap-tap-."

The clatter of high heels on bare board floor, muted by walls in between, fades away into nothingness. An aching emptiness of sound falls on the ears of the listeners below stairs. Interminable seconds drip away into minutes, endless minutes draw tension until the hum of a fly is the roar of a motor.

In the dim light the door is seen to swing gently. A slight creak at the hinges brings the watchers to the sharpest attention. Upstairs, a chair scrapes gently across the floor, goes over with a crash. The skeptical watchers spring to their feet. The lights flash on.

"Tap-tap-tap-tap-."

The clatter of high heels on a bare board floor fades away, then vanishes.

The ghost has walked again.

Nerves Being Shattered

Such is the story in and about Nanuet and unless the ghost is laid with proper incantations very shortly there will be no sleep o'nights for householders with unsteady nerves.

Rockland County has few authentic haunted houses and Nanuet none at all unless its present claims to distinction stands up under close scrutiny. The story has all the earmarks of authenticity and background is there in abundance.

On the Nyack Turnpike, as it used to run west of Nanuet and just beyond the intersection of the two and three-strip concrete, stands the house owned by Emil Freedman.

(The remainder of this article was not available. However, a follow-up article appeared two days later.)

Journal News
Monday, January 31, 1938

Spook Haunts Nanuet House in Vain Effort to Do Convincing Job

Nanuet is still in a dither. No rank realist has this far come along to spoil things completely, yet that seems to be what will happen and the village may yet have an honest-to-gosh bonafide haunted house, something to which no other community in the county can lay legitimate claim. There have been so many hushed discussions of the possibilities and there is so much bated breath that a poor fish doesn't have a chance.

Even those stalwart minions of law and order in Clarkstown, Walter Liebert and Ray Lindeman, are still completely in the dark over this startling case and their hands close on emptiness as they strike desperately to come to grips with mortal conflict with miasmas and phatasmogorias. If P.T. Barnum were only in circulation hereabouts he would have an attraction for his greatest show on earth this year that "walks and talks and screams and yells and crawls on its belly like a reptile." Nobody can gainsay the claim for nobody has seen the spook. But it has been heard—and how!

It's a new accomplishment for the house so far as the owner, Emil Freedman, is concerned and he expresses the greatest doubt over the authenticity of all the haunting. He and his family lived there for a number of years and not once was there the least disturbance. The police, the realists that they are, grin with the greatest circumspection for they too are from Missouri. [The Show Me state.] *The proverbial grain of salt with them would now pass for a full pound.*

The curious and the credulous are still greatly interested and the story continues on its merry way. Mrs. Miller, thinking it might be errant squirrels or inquisitive rats, put out nuts and rat poison but both went untouched and the noises continued. Now she lean toward the belief that somebody with a practical joke in mind has a hidden wire installed to connect to some sort of loud speaker in the walls but it's not her idea of a joke.

Mr. Freedman is naturally not greatly pleased with the ghost supposition and it is most reasonable to suppose that the haunt will vanish to the same dim beyond as the West Nyack wampus [large cat-like creature] *which jumped from bog to bog and then bogged down again last Fall.*

Doesn't Believe in Ghosts

A Journal-News reporter has made an exhaustive investigation, discussing the matter with both the owner and Mrs. William Martin, tenant in the house. The latter told of hearing "sounds and voices from the attic and shrieks of a woman's voice," and that other strange noises sounded through the house at night.

The reporter asked if he might investigate, but Mrs. Martin declared that it would do no good to look into the matter until nightfall. In answer to an offer to come and spend an evening in the attic, Mrs. Martin said that she was "too nervous." When asked if she believed in ghosts, Mrs. Martin replied in the negative emphatically.

Mr. Freedman, however, said that the whole story was ridiculous in that he had lived next door and never heard a sound except for chickens scratching near the rear porch. The house, Mr. Freedman said, was erected ten years ago and for nine years he has not had a single complaint from the two tenants that occupied it during that period. He said that he hoped no one would take the stories seriously since he said he felt it would be unjust to any tenant who might later occupy the premises, if fantastic tales were to circulate.

"Of course, it would be nice to laugh off the whole thing as silly but at the same time I have an investment to protect and it might do me great harm if the matter of renting or selling if the fantastic tale were not denied," he said.

Mrs. Martin says she expects to move February 1 and after that date Mr. Freedman plans to repair and renovate throughout. He doesn't expect to unearth any spooks.

Copy this page to use for your own ghost hunt. If you know of a haunted site you think should be considered for an upcoming book, please contact me at:

P.O. Box 192, Blooming Grove, NY, 10914

www.ghostinvestigator.com

Field Report

Date: **Location:**

Time In: **Weather:**

Names of People Interviewed:

Equipment: Camera □ **Video** □ **Audio Recorder**
□ **Thermometer**   **Other:**

Experiences: Sounds □   **Odors** □   **Cold Spots** □

Visuals □ **Touch/Sensations** □ **Movement** □

Details (Attach extra sheet if necessary):

Time Out: **Total Time on Site:**

Conclusions:

Prepared and Signed by:

Witness(es):

Other books by Linda Zimmermann
Available in print and as e-books
For more info and to order autographed copies:
www.gotozim.com

Dead Center
A Ghost Hunter Novel

When one of the country's largest shopping centers is built in Virginia, rumors abound that the place is haunted by ghosts of Civil War soldiers. Ghost hunter Sarah Brooks must uncover the truth, and come face to face with the restless spirits that walk through the *Dead Center*:

Okay, Sarah Brooks. This is what you do, she said to herself. *This is who you are.*

Closing her eyes, Sarah spun around and counted to three. When she opened her eyes, she had to clamp her hand over her mouth to stifle a scream. There was a pale, misty shape of a man drawing closer. It was like an image being projected into a fog, and it rippled, wavered, then slowly began to take on a more defined shape. The wounded man behind her screamed as if Death himself was coming to take him…

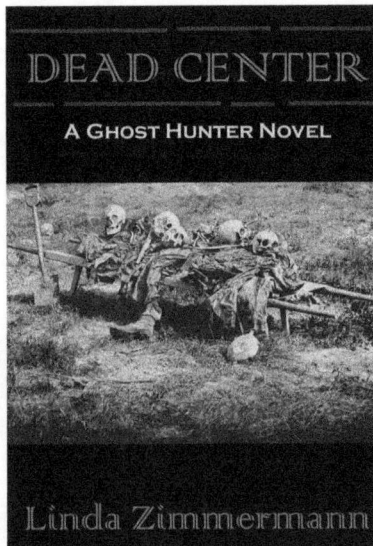

Ghost Investigator Series

Ghost Investigator Volume 1:
Hauntings of the Hudson Valley

Ghost Investigator Volume 2:
From Gettysburg to Lizzie Borden

Ghost Investigator Volume 3

Ghost Investigator Volume 4:
Ghosts of New York and New Jersey

Ghost Investigator Volume 5:
From Beyond the Grave

Ghost Investigator Volume 6:
Dark Shadows

Ghost Investigator Volume 7:
Psychic Impressions

Ghost Investigator Volume 8:
Back Into the Light

Ghost Investigator Volume 9:
Back from the Dead

Ghost Investigator Volume 10

Ghost Investigator 10th Anniversary Special Edition:
Favorite Haunts

Ghosts of Rockland County:
Collected Stories Edition

Hudson Valley Haunts:
Historic Driving Tours

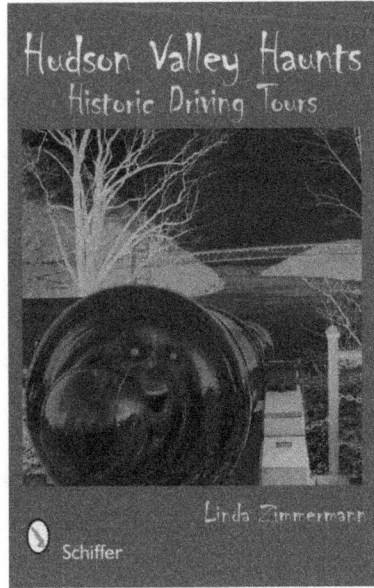

New York's Hudson River Valley is a place of captivating beauty and fascinating history. It is also one of the most haunted regions in the country. From ancient Indian spirits at Spook Rock, to soldiers still walking the battlefield of Fort Montgomery, to the many haunted houses that line the streets of the old Dutch settlements in New Paltz and Hurley, this book has something extra to offer tourists—ghosts that still make their presence known to those who dare to visit.

What greater adventure can there be then to go to such a site, explore the rich history of its people and the events, and then see if you can discover any deeper secrets from the other world, where a passing shadow or faint whisper may signal that you have just had an encounter in the haunted Hudson Valley.

America's Historic Haunts

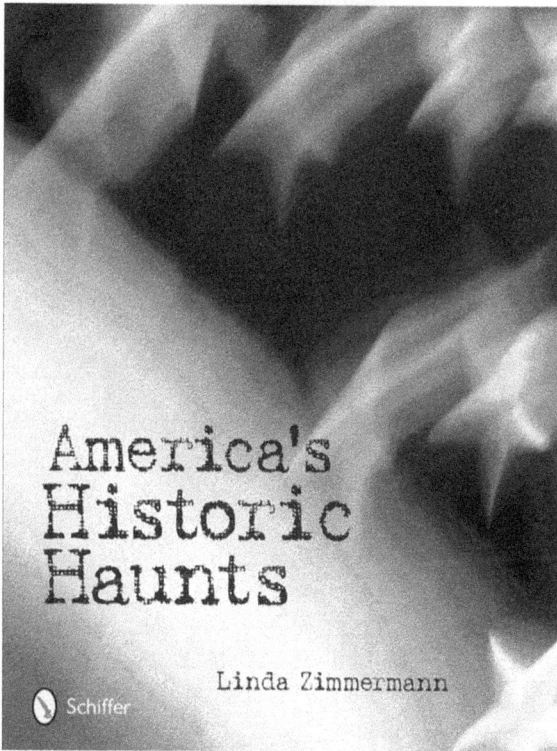

From remote villages in Alaska, to ancient Native American settlements in the southwest, to an old Spanish town in Florida, and bustling metropolitan areas in the northeast, follow the fascinating trail of historic haunts across the country. Test your ghost hunting skills in an old prison or fort, dine in restaurants where paranormal activity is on the menu, and sleep in some of America's most haunted inns. Whether you're a frequent flier or an armchair adventurer, this book will take you on a journey of discovery into the people, places, and events that led to the spirits that still walk among us in some of this country's greatest travel destinations.

HVZA:
Hudson Valley Zombie Apocalypse

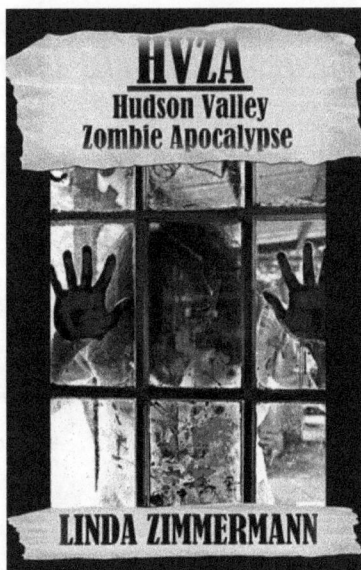

Amazon.com Reviews:

"GREAT book. Buy it; you won't regret it. Well... except maybe for at 3 AM when you're either A) still up reading because can't put this page-turner down or B) waking up out of a zombie nightmare because the characters and situations in the book can seem so REAL. But buy it anyway."

"You relate, you get sucked in, seriously it's been a while since I enjoyed a book so much."

"The author has an uncanny ability to pull you into the story and make you feel like you are there."

"Zimmermann really hits home with her depiction of life during the collapse of civilization, and the heart wrenching losses, choices and sacrifices that people must make in order to survive. Zimmermann is a master manipulator of emotions: the love, fear, sadness, pain, and suffering of the various characters are surprisingly real. Set in the Hudson Valley, the authentic locations and settings lend an additional layer of realism that so many other works of fiction neglect. These just are not zombies that are attacking people - these are zombies that are attacking your neighbors and family and friends."

Bad Science:
A Brief History of Bizarre Misconceptions, Totally Wrong Conclusions, and Incredibly Stupid Theories

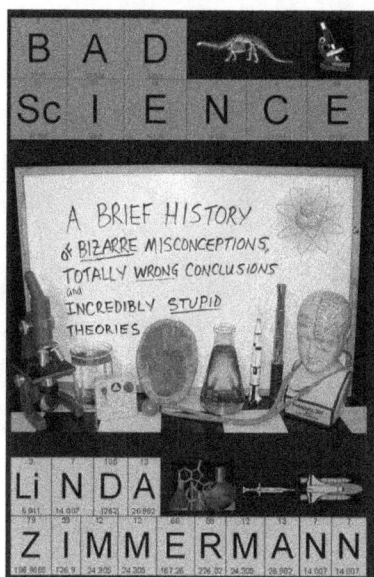

Winner of the 2011 Silver Medal for Humor
in the international Independent Publisher Awards

Amazon.com Review:

"*Bad Science* is simultaneously informative and ever-so-entertaining. Riveting! Enthralling! Hilarious! I highly recommend this book if you like a jaw dropping read that is a LAUGH OUT LOUD."

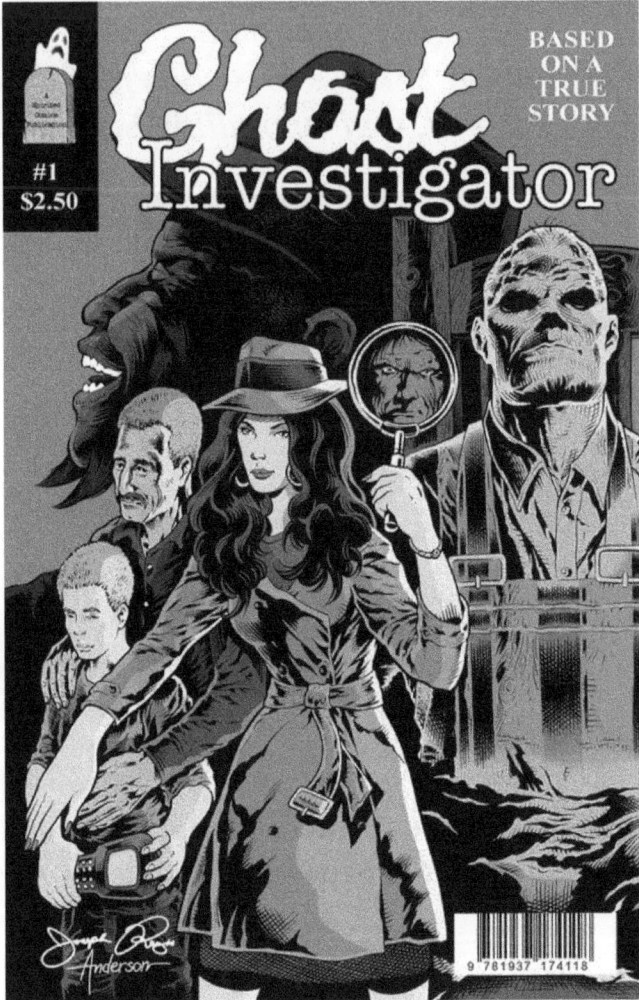

Ghost Investigator
The Comic Book
Issue #1

Available at: www.comicfleamarket.com

HVZA:
Hudson Valley Zombie Apocalypse

THE GRAPHIC NOVEL

HVZA
Hudson Valley Zombie Apocalypse

Based on the novel by
Linda Zimmermann
Project Director
Don E. Smith, Jr.
Art Director & Cover
Nick Mockoviak

"A truly imaginative Zombie Anthology. Full of stories for every appetite."
- Paul J. Salamoff
Writer/Producer

"A truly imaginative Zombie Anthology. Full of stories for every appetite."
-- Paul J. Salamoff, Writer/Producer (Discord, Logan's Run: Last Day)

"Not since peanut butter and chocolate has there been as perfect a combination as zombies and comics! What's better than one zombie story? How about a whole brain-eating collection of zombie stories?!"
--Jim Salicrup, Editor-in-Chief, Papercutz and former Marvel Comics editor on "The Avengers," "The Amazing Spider-Man," "The Uncanny X-Men" and "The Fantastic Four."

In the Night Sky
Hudson Valley UFO Sightings
from the 1930s to the Present

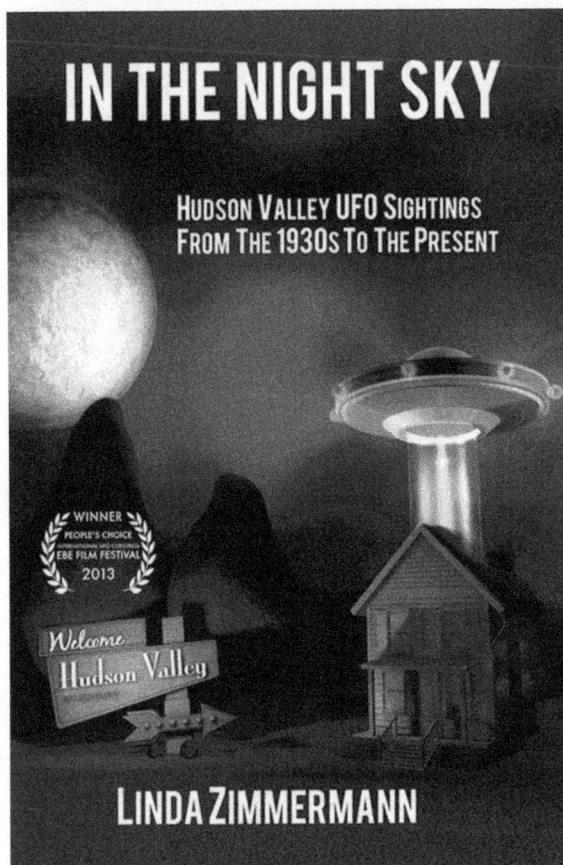

IN THE NIGHT SKY

HUDSON VALLEY UFO SIGHTINGS
FROM THE 1930S TO THE PRESENT

WINNER
PEOPLE'S CHOICE
EBE FILM FESTIVAL
2013

Welcome
Hudson Valley

LINDA ZIMMERMANN

Eyewitness accounts of classic flying saucers, giant, silent triangles, and possible abductions in one of the most active UFO areas of the country.

The film based on the book was the winner of the People's Choice Award at the EBE Film Festival at the 2013 International UFO Congress.

www.ingramcontent.com/pod-product-compliance
Lightning Source LLC
Chambersburg PA
CBHW030020290326
41934CB00005B/412